GUTS, GRACE & GRIT

Your Guide to Navigating Weight-loss Surgery

Juanita Renee Burgess

Table Of Contents

Introduction

Weight loss surgery changes everything, and nobody talks about the real stuff that happens inside your head and heart when you make this choice. The doctors give you pamphlets about vitamins and protein shakes, but they don't tell you how to handle your sister who keeps saying you're taking the easy way out, or how to quiet that voice in your head that whispers you don't deserve this chance at a new life.

You picked up this book because something inside you knows you need more than medical facts and food lists.

Maybe you've spent months reading every article online, joining Facebook groups, and asking the same questions over and over because you're scared you'll mess this up like you've messed up every diet before. Maybe you've had the consultation, scheduled the surgery, and now you're lying awake at night wondering if you're making the biggest mistake of your life or the best decision you've ever made. The truth sits somewhere in the middle of all that fear and hope, and that's exactly where we're going to meet you.

This book exists because weight loss surgery isn't just about your stomach getting smaller. Your whole world shifts, and the people around you react in ways that shock you, support you, or sometimes try to sabotage you without even knowing they're doing it. You need tools for all of it, not just the part that happens in the operating room.

Welcome to Your Transformation Journey

Right now, you're standing at the edge of something huge, and that takes guts most people will never understand. You've probably been heavy for years, maybe decades, and you've tried everything from juice cleanses to personal trainers to meal delivery services that cost more than your car payment. You've lost weight and gained it back so many times that you've stopped believing you can actually succeed at anything related to your body.

Then someone mentioned surgery, or maybe you researched it yourself after another failed attempt at losing weight the "normal" way.

The idea scared you and excited you at the same time because finally, here was something that might actually work, something that could give you the life you've been dreaming about while you've been hiding in oversized clothes and avoiding cameras. But along with that hope came a flood of new fears, and suddenly you weren't just worried about failing at another diet, you were worried about failing at surgery, about complications, about loose skin, about your marriage surviving your transformation, about your kids seeing you differently, about becoming someone you don't recognize.

Those fears make sense because this decision affects everything.

When you change your relationship with food, you change your relationship with comfort, with stress, with celebration, with grief, and with every emotion you've been managing with eating for as long as you can remember. When you start losing weight quickly, people notice, and they have opinions, and some of those opinions feel like attacks on choices you're making to save your own life. When you can't eat the way you used to, family dinners become complicated, work lunches become awkward, and you realize how much of your social life revolved around food.

This journey requires three things that nobody teaches you how to develop: guts to make hard choices when everyone around you has opinions about your body, grace to forgive yourself when you're not perfect and to handle other people's reactions with kindness instead of anger, and grit to keep going when the honeymoon phase ends and you realize that surgery fixed your stomach but you still have to do the work of building a life you love.

You already have these qualities inside you, even if you don't feel them right now. The fact that you're here, reading this, researching surgery, considering such a big change despite all your fears, proves you have more courage than you give yourself credit for. You've survived everything that brought you to this point, every cruel comment about your weight, every time you felt invisible or ashamed, every diet that promised everything and delivered nothing, every doctor who made you feel like your weight was a moral failing instead of a complex medical issue.

You're still here, still fighting for a better life, still believing somewhere deep down that you deserve to feel good in your body and show up fully in your life. That's not weakness, that's strength, and it's exactly what you need to succeed at this.

Why Is This Book for You?

Most books about weight loss surgery read like medical textbooks or cheerleading sessions, and neither one helps you when you're crying in your car after someone asks if you've considered just eating less and moving more. This book comes from someone who has lived through the whole experience, from the first scary Google search about surgery to years later when people who knew you before don't recognize you and you sometimes don't recognize yourself. The difference is in the details nobody talks about.

Like how to respond when your coworker says surgery is cheating, or when your mother-in-law starts bringing your favorite dessert to every family gathering after you've told her you can't eat sugar anymore, or when your spouse starts acting weird because you're getting attention from strangers and they're not sure how they feel about sharing you with a world that used to ignore you. Like how to handle the grief that comes with letting go of food as your primary comfort, or the strange guilt you feel when you realize losing weight is actually easier after surgery than it ever was before, or the fear that creeps in when you think about what happens if you gain the weight back. These are the real challenges that determine whether surgery changes your life or just changes your pants size.

The medical team prepares your body for surgery, but nobody prepares your mind and heart for everything that comes after. You need strategies for handling jealous friends who start making comments about how you think you're better than everyone now that you're losing weight. You need scripts for responding to people who want to debate the safety of surgery or tell you about their cousin who had complications. You need tools for building confidence that doesn't depend on the number on the scale, because weight loss stalls and plateaus and sometimes the scale goes up even when you're doing everything right.

However, you don't need permission to take up space and set boundaries with people who think your body is their business.

This guide gives you real-world wisdom from someone who has coached dozens of people through their own transformations and seen countless possible scenarios play out. You'll learn how to identify sabotage before it derails your progress, how to build a support system that actually supports you instead of undermining your success, and how to develop unshakeable confidence that survives criticism, plateaus, and all the ups and downs that come with changing your entire life.

The approach here focuses on progress over perfection, self-compassion over self-criticism, and building a life you love instead of just losing weight. Because surgery is a tool, not a magic wand, and your success depends on how well you learn to use that tool while dealing with everything else that comes with transformation.

Your Roadmap to Guts, Grace & Grit

This book covers everything from the moment you start considering surgery to years after when you're living in your new body and helping other people find their own courage. We start with the mental preparation that nobody talks about, the work you need to do before surgery to set yourself up for long-term success instead of just short-term weight loss.

You'll learn how to silence your inner critic, that voice that tells you you're not worth the investment, that you'll probably fail anyway, that you should just try harder to lose weight naturally even though you've been trying harder for years without lasting results.

We'll cover how to handle every type of reaction from family and friends, from the people who worry about your safety to the people who resent your success to the people who suddenly want to be your best friend now that you're losing weight. You'll get specific scripts for responding to comments about taking the easy way out, about surgery being dangerous, about how you look too thin or you're losing weight too fast or you're getting obsessed with your appearance.

The section on building unshakeable confidence teaches you how to separate your worth from your weight, how to celebrate victories that have nothing to do with the scale, and how to handle the inevitable plateaus and stalls without spiraling into old patterns of self-criticism and giving up. You'll learn how to dress your changing body, how to handle compliments without deflecting them, and how to show up in photos and social situations with confidence instead of hiding.

We'll talk about the relationship changes that nobody warns you about, how weight loss affects marriages and friendships and family dynamics in ways that surprise everyone involved.

You'll get tools for maintaining intimacy with your partner while you're both adjusting to your new body and new confidence, strategies for dealing with friends who feel threatened by your transformation, and ways to handle family members who try to sabotage your progress because your success makes them uncomfortable about their own choices.

The practical sections cover everything from navigating restaurants and social events to traveling with your new eating requirements to handling holidays and celebrations that used to revolve around food. You'll learn how to meal prep efficiently, how to get enough protein without getting bored, how to handle cravings and emotional eating triggers, and how to build new coping strategies that don't involve food.

Throughout everything, we focus on developing grit, the ability to keep going when motivation fades and the novelty wears off and you realize that surgery solved some problems but created new challenges you didn't expect. You'll learn how to bounce back from mistakes without turning them into complete derailments, how to adjust your approach when something isn't working, and how to maintain your progress for years instead of just months.

This roadmap takes you from scared and uncertain to confident and capable, from hiding behind your weight to showing up fully in your life, from letting other people's opinions control your choices to making decisions based on what's best for your health and happiness. The journey isn't always easy, but it's worth it, and you're worth it, and by the time you finish this book, you'll believe that too.

Chapter 1: A Life-Changing Decision

The moment you start seriously considering weight loss surgery, everything shifts inside your head. You're not just thinking about losing weight anymore, you're thinking about changing your entire life, and that realization hits you like a truck some random Tuesday when you're scrolling through before and after photos on Instagram or reading success stories in a Facebook group.

This isn't another diet you can quit when it gets hard. Surgery means making a permanent change to your body, and once you cross that line, there's no going back to the way things were before. The finality of that decision scares you and thrills you at the same time because finally, here's something that might actually work, but also, what if you're not ready for everything that comes with it.

Most people spend months or even years in this space between wanting surgery and actually scheduling it, and that's completely normal. You're not just deciding to have a medical procedure, you're deciding to become a different version of yourself, and that requires courage most people will never understand. The research phase feels safer than the commitment phase because you can always tell yourself you're just exploring options, just gathering information, just seeing what's out there.

But somewhere along the way, exploring turns into planning, and planning turns into scheduling, and suddenly you have a surgery date and you're wondering how you got here and whether you're making the right choice.

The truth is, there's never a perfect time to have surgery, and you're never going to feel completely ready for such a big change. The decision happens when staying the same becomes more uncomfortable than facing the unknown, when the life you're living feels smaller than the life you know you could have, when the fear of remaining stuck outweighs the fear of transformation.

Facing the Mirror Moment

The mirror moment doesn't always happen in front of an actual mirror. Sometimes it happens when you're looking at photos from a family gathering and barely recognize yourself, or when you realize you've been avoiding activities you used to love because your body can't keep up anymore, or when your doctor starts using words like diabetes and high blood pressure and sleep apnea in the same sentence as your name.

For some people, the mirror moment is dramatic, like not fitting in an airplane seat or breaking a chair or having a health scare that forces them to confront their mortality.

For others, it's quieter, more subtle, like realizing you've been living your life on the sidelines, watching other people do things you wish you could do, making excuses for why you can't participate fully in your own life. Maybe you stopped going to the beach because you hate how you look in a bathing suit, or you avoid dancing at weddings because you're self-conscious about your size, or you decline invitations because you're worried about fitting in restaurant booths or having enough energy to keep up with the group.

The mirror moment is when you stop making excuses and start admitting the truth about how your weight affects your quality of life, your relationships, your career, your health, and your happiness. It's when you acknowledge that all the diets you've tried, all the exercise programs you've started and stopped, all the promises you've made to yourself about eating better and moving more haven't created lasting change, and you need something different.

This realization feels like failure at first, like admitting defeat, like giving up on your ability to solve this problem on your own. You might feel ashamed that you need surgery when other people seem to lose weight just by cutting out soda or joining a gym. You might worry that choosing surgery means you're weak or lazy or taking the easy way out.

Those feelings are normal, but they're not accurate. Recognizing that you need a tool to help you succeed doesn't make you weak, it makes you smart. Admitting that willpower alone hasn't worked for you doesn't mean you lack character, it means you understand that obesity is a complex medical condition that often requires medical intervention. Choosing surgery means you're done accepting a life that feels too small for who you really are.

The mirror moment is actually a moment of clarity and courage. You're looking at your life honestly, without the filters and excuses and someday thinking that has kept you stuck in patterns that don't serve you. You're acknowledging that you deserve better than what you've been accepting, that your dreams and goals matter enough to take dramatic action, that your health and happiness are worth the risk and investment and hard work that surgery requires.

When you reach this point, write it down. Document exactly how you're feeling, what prompted this realization, what you hope surgery will make possible in your life. This becomes part of your why, your anchor when doubt creeps in later, your reminder of what motivated you to make such a big decision. The mirror moment is powerful because it cuts through all the noise and gets to the heart of what really matters: you want your life back, and you're willing to do what it takes to get it.

Separating Facts from Fear

Once you start researching weight loss surgery, you'll find more information than you know what to do with, and not all of it is helpful or accurate. The internet is full of horror stories, miracle transformations, outdated statistics, and conflicting advice that can paralyze you with fear or give you unrealistic expectations about what surgery can and can't do.

Your job is to separate legitimate concerns from fear-based thinking, medical facts from opinion pieces, current information from outdated studies, and realistic expectations from fantasy outcomes.

Start with reputable medical sources like the American Society for Metabolic and Bariatric Surgery, major medical centers that perform these procedures regularly, and peer-reviewed research studies rather than blog posts and forum discussions. While patient experiences can be valuable for understanding the emotional and practical aspects of surgery, they shouldn't be your primary source of medical information.

Every surgery carries risks, and weight loss surgery is no exception. The key is understanding what those risks actually are, how often they occur, and how they compare to the risks of remaining significantly overweight. Most people focus intensely on surgical risks while completely ignoring the very real risks of obesity, like heart disease, stroke, diabetes, sleep apnea, joint problems, and certain types of cancer.

The mortality rate for weight loss surgery is extremely low, comparable to gallbladder surgery, and significantly lower than the long-term mortality risk of severe obesity. Serious complications occur in less than five percent of cases, and most of them are treatable when they do happen. These statistics matter because fear often magnifies risks while minimizing benefits, leading to decisions based on emotion rather than evidence.

When you read horror stories online, remember that people are much more likely to post about negative experiences than positive ones. The thousands of people who have successful surgery and go on to live healthier, happier lives aren't usually writing detailed posts about their ordinary, wonderful outcomes. They're too busy living their lives to spend time on forums describing how well everything went.

Pay attention to the source and timing of the information you're reading. Surgery techniques have improved dramatically over the past decade, complication rates have decreased, and long-term success rates have increased. A study from 2010 doesn't reflect current practices and outcomes. An article written by someone who had surgery fifteen years ago doesn't represent today's experience.

Focus on finding a qualified surgeon who performs your chosen procedure regularly, works at an accredited center, and has good outcomes data. Ask about their complication rates, revision rates, and long-term success statistics. A good surgeon will be transparent about risks and realistic about expectations while also helping you understand the benefits and potential for improved quality of life.

Don't let perfect be the enemy of good when it comes to research. You'll never know everything, and there will always be more studies to read, more opinions to consider, more what-if scenarios to worry about. At some point, you have enough information to make an informed decision, and continuing to research becomes a way to avoid making that decision rather than preparing for it.

Trust yourself to weigh the risks and benefits based on your specific situation, your health history, your quality of life goals, and your willingness to make the lifestyle changes that surgery requires. The decision is ultimately yours, and you're the only one who knows whether the potential benefits outweigh the risks in your particular circumstances.

Permission to Choose Yourself

The hardest part of deciding on weight loss surgery often isn't the medical concerns or the lifestyle changes or even the financial investment. The hardest part is giving yourself permission to choose your health and happiness over other people's opinions, expectations, and comfort levels.

You've probably spent years, maybe decades, putting everyone else's needs before your own, and now you're considering a major decision that's entirely about you and what you need to live a better life.

This feels selfish because you've been conditioned to believe that taking care of yourself is less important than taking care of everyone around you. You worry about the cost, even though you've spent thousands of dollars on your family's needs without question. You worry about taking time off work for surgery and recovery, even though you've used vacation days for everyone else's emergencies and appointments. You worry about asking for help during your recovery, even though you've been helping everyone else with their challenges for years.

The guilt runs deeper than practical concerns. You feel guilty for wanting to look better, as if vanity is a character flaw rather than a normal human desire to feel confident and attractive. You feel guilty for spending money on yourself, as if your health and happiness are less worthy of investment than your children's activities or your home improvements or your spouse's hobbies.

You feel guilty for not being able to lose weight on your own, as if needing help is a moral failing rather than a practical decision to use an effective tool. This guilt serves no one, including the people you think you're protecting by putting their needs first. When you don't take care of yourself, you can't show up fully for the people you love. When you're unhappy with your body and your health, that unhappiness affects your relationships, your parenting, your work performance, and every aspect of your life. When you model self-sacrifice and self-neglect, you teach the people around you that their own needs don't matter either.

Choosing surgery is choosing to model self-care and self-advocacy. You're showing your children that their health matters enough to take dramatic action when necessary. You're showing your spouse that you value your relationship enough to invest in becoming the healthiest, happiest version of yourself. You're showing your friends and family that you believe you deserve to feel good in your body and participate fully in life.

The people who truly love you want you to be healthy and happy, even if they're scared about surgery or worried about how your transformation might affect your relationship with them. The people who don't support your decision to prioritize your health are revealing more about their own issues than about the validity of your choice.

You don't need anyone's permission to make decisions about your own body, but you do need to give yourself permission to make those decisions without guilt or apology. Your body belongs to you, your health affects you more than anyone else, and your happiness matters just as much as everyone else's happiness.

Surgery isn't giving up, it's gearing up. It's not taking the easy way out, it's taking the way that works. It's not admitting failure, it's choosing success. You're not broken and in need of fixing, you're strong and worthy of having the life you want.

The permission you're looking for has to come from you, not from your family, your friends, your coworkers, or random people on the internet who have opinions about weight loss surgery. You're the only one who knows what it's like to live in your body, to deal with your health issues, to navigate your daily challenges, to dream your dreams and wonder if you'll ever feel confident enough to pursue them.

Give yourself permission to want more than what you have now. Give yourself permission to use every tool available to create the life you want. Give yourself permission to choose yourself, finally and completely, without apology or explanation or justification to anyone else.

Your Why Becomes Your Anchor

Your why is the reason you're willing to have surgery, change your entire relationship with food, deal with other people's opinions, and rebuild your life around new habits and priorities. This why needs to be deeper than wanting to look good in a bathing suit or fitting into smaller clothes, because those surface-level motivations won't sustain you through the challenging parts of this journey.

The real why usually connects to how you want to feel in your body and what you want to be able to do with your life that feels impossible right now. Maybe your why is wanting to keep up with your children without getting winded, or traveling without worrying about fitting in airplane seats, or going to your high school reunion without feeling self-conscious, or hiking that trail you've been talking about for years, or dancing at your daughter's wedding without worrying about how you look in photos. Maybe it's about reducing your diabetes medication or getting off blood pressure pills or sleeping through the night without a CPAP machine.

Your why might be about confidence and self-worth, about finally feeling comfortable in your own skin, about shopping in regular stores instead of plus-size sections, about wearing sleeveless shirts in summer or going to the pool with your kids or trying activities you've been avoiding because of your weight. Maybe you want to feel attractive again, to see desire in your partner's eyes, to believe you're worthy of love and attention and respect regardless of your size.

Some people's why is about longevity, about being around for their grandchildren, about aging gracefully instead of struggling with mobility and health issues, about having energy for the things that matter most to them. Others are motivated by career goals, social opportunities, or simply the desire to stop thinking about their weight every single day and focus their mental energy on more important things.

Your why is personal and specific to your life, your dreams, your values, and your circumstances. It doesn't have to make sense to anyone else, and it doesn't have to be noble or inspiring or politically correct. It just has to be true for you and powerful enough to motivate you through the difficult parts of this process.

Write down your why in detail, not just the surface reason but the deeper emotional truth underneath it. If you want to lose weight to feel more confident, dig deeper and ask what confidence would make possible in your life. If you want surgery to improve your health, be specific about what health improvements would mean for your daily experience, your relationships, your future plans. The more specific and emotional your why becomes, the more powerful it will be when you need it most.

You'll need your why when you're in the pre-surgery liquid diet phase and feeling hungry and cranky and wondering if you've made a terrible mistake. You'll need it when you're recovering from surgery and everything hurts and you can barely eat anything and you're questioning whether this was worth it. You'll need it when the weight loss slows down and you hit your first plateau and start wondering if surgery is working for you.

You'll need your why when people make comments about how you look too thin or you're losing weight too fast or you should eat more because you're getting obsessed with your diet. You'll need it when friends start acting weird around you because you can't eat the way you used to, or when family members make passive-aggressive comments about your new lifestyle, or when strangers feel entitled to comment on your transformation.

Your why anchors you to your decision when doubt creeps in, when progress stalls, when other people's opinions start affecting your confidence, when the novelty wears off and you realize that surgery is just the beginning of a lifelong commitment to different choices. It reminds you that this journey is about more than weight loss, it's about reclaiming your life and becoming the person you've always known you could be.

Keep your why visible and accessible. Write it down and put it somewhere you'll see it regularly. Record yourself reading it out loud so you can listen to it when you need encouragement. Share it with supportive people who can remind you of it when you forget. Update it as your motivations evolve and your goals become reality.

Your why is your North Star, your constant reminder of what this journey is really about and why you decided it was worth the risk, the investment, the hard work, and the courage it takes to transform your entire life.

Chapter 1 Make Your Move

These exercises help you clarify your decision, document your motivations, and prepare mentally for the journey ahead. Complete them honestly and thoroughly, because the work you do now creates the foundation for everything that comes later.

First, write your mirror moment story. Describe the specific moment, event, or realization that made you seriously consider weight loss surgery. Include details about how you felt, what you were thinking, what you realized about your current situation, and what you hoped surgery might make possible. This story becomes part of your permanent record, a reminder of what motivated you to take action when staying the same became more uncomfortable than facing change.

Next, create your comprehensive why statement. Start

with the surface reasons you want surgery, then dig deeper into the emotional and lifestyle motivations underneath those reasons. Ask yourself what each benefit would make possible in your life, how it would change your daily experience, what dreams it would help you pursue. Write at least three paragraphs, getting more specific and emotional with each one.

Complete a fear versus fact analysis by making two columns on a piece of paper. In the first column, list every fear you have about surgery, from medical complications to social consequences to personal concerns. In the second column, research and write the actual facts related to each fear, including statistics, current medical information, and realistic assessments of likelihood and severity.

Document your current quality of life by listing specific ways your weight currently limits your activities, affects your health, impacts your relationships, or prevents you from pursuing goals and dreams. Be honest about physical limitations, emotional challenges, social situations you avoid, and opportunities you've passed up because of weight-related concerns.

Write a letter to yourself from your future self, five years after successful surgery. Describe what your life looks like, how you feel in your body, what you're able to do that you can't do now, how your relationships have improved, what goals you've accomplished. Make this letter specific and positive, focusing on the life you're working toward rather than just the weight you want to lose.

Create a support system assessment by listing the people in your life and categorizing them as supporters, skeptics, or saboteurs based on their likely reaction to your surgery decision. Identify who you can count on for encouragement, who might need education about your choice, and who you might need to limit contact with during your transformation.

Finally, establish your decision timeline by setting specific dates for important milestones like choosing a surgeon, attending information sessions, completing required medical evaluations, and scheduling surgery if you decide to proceed. Having concrete deadlines prevents endless research and procrastination while ensuring you take the necessary steps at an appropriate pace.

Keep all of these documents in a journal or folder that you can reference throughout your journey. These exercises create clarity about your motivations, help you make an informed decision, and provide encouragement when you need reminders about why you chose this path.

Chapter 2: Silencing the Critics (Including the One in Your Head)

The voice in your head starts talking the moment you seriously consider weight loss surgery, and it rarely has anything nice to say. It whispers that you're not disciplined enough to succeed, that you're taking the easy way out, that you'll probably fail at this just like you've failed at every diet before, that you don't deserve to invest this much money and effort in yourself when other people in your life have needs too.

This inner critic gets louder when other people start sharing their opinions about your decision.

Your coworker mentions her friend's cousin who had complications from surgery. Your mother-in-law asks why you can't just eat less and exercise more like she did back in her day. Your neighbor starts sending you articles about natural weight loss methods and success stories of people who lost weight without surgery. Everyone suddenly becomes an expert on your body, your health, and your choices, and their voices join the chorus of doubt already playing in your head.

The combination of internal self-criticism and external judgment can paralyze you with doubt, make you question your decision, or convince you to postpone surgery indefinitely while you try one more diet, one more exercise program, one more attempt at losing weight naturally. But here's what nobody tells you about criticism: it usually says more about the person giving it than about the validity of your choice, and learning to handle it effectively is one of the most important skills you can develop for this journey.

Silencing critics doesn't mean making them disappear or convincing everyone to support your decision. It means developing the mental tools to protect your confidence, maintain your resolve, and make choices based on what's best for your health and happiness rather than what makes other people comfortable.

The Inner Critic's Greatest Hits

Your inner critic has been practicing its routine for years, maybe decades, and it knows exactly which buttons to push to make you feel ashamed, guilty, or unworthy of success. The thoughts feel so automatic and familiar that you might not even recognize them as criticism rather than facts, but learning to identify these patterns is the first step to changing them.

The "not good enough" track plays on repeat, telling you that you're not disciplined enough, strong enough, or deserving enough to succeed at surgery when you've failed at everything else. This voice reminds you of every diet you've quit, every gym membership you've wasted, every promise you've broken to yourself about eating better and exercising more. It suggests that surgery won't work for you because you lack the willpower and commitment that successful people have.

The "what will people think" soundtrack focuses on other people's opinions and judgments, imagining scenarios where friends, family members, coworkers, or even strangers criticize your decision to have surgery. This voice predicts that people will think you're lazy, vain, weak, or irresponsible for choosing surgery instead of losing weight naturally. It worries about being judged at family gatherings, work events, or social situations where your eating habits will be different.

The "too expensive and selfish" melody plays guilt about spending money on yourself, taking time off work for surgery and recovery, asking family members for help during your healing process, or prioritizing your health over other people's needs and wants. This voice suggests that the money could be better spent on your children's education, home improvements, or family vacations, and that focusing on your appearance and health is vanity rather than self-care.

The "what if something goes wrong" chorus amplifies every possible risk, complication, or negative outcome associated with surgery while completely ignoring the risks of remaining significantly overweight. This voice focuses on horror stories, worst-case scenarios, and statistical outliers while dismissing the high success rates and improved quality of life that most people experience after surgery.

The "you'll probably gain it back anyway" refrain predicts failure before you even begin, reminding you of past weight loss attempts that didn't last and suggesting that surgery will be just another temporary fix. This voice tells you that you don't have what it takes to maintain the lifestyle changes that surgery requires, that you'll eventually return to old eating habits, and that you'll end up heavier than you started.

These thoughts feel true because they're familiar and because they tap into real fears and insecurities that most people carry about their weight, their worth, and their ability to change. But familiarity doesn't equal accuracy, and the fact that you've thought something repeatedly doesn't make it a fact about your character, your capabilities, or your likelihood of success.

Your brain defaults to fear and negativity as a survival mechanism, trying to protect you from perceived threats like rejection, failure, or physical harm. The inner critic thinks it's helping by preparing you for the worst-case scenario, but in reality, it's often preventing you from taking action that could dramatically improve your life. Understanding why these thoughts exist helps you recognize them as mental habits rather than truths about your situation. You can acknowledge the thoughts without believing them, thank your brain for trying to protect you, and then choose to focus on more accurate and helpful perspectives that support your goals rather than sabotage them.

The inner critic loses power when you stop treating its commentary as gospel truth and start treating it as background noise that you can choose to ignore. You don't have to argue with these thoughts or prove them wrong, you just have to stop letting them make your decisions for you.

Rewriting Your Internal Script

Changing the way you talk to yourself requires conscious effort and consistent practice, but it's one of the most powerful things you can do to support your success with weight loss surgery. The goal isn't to become unrealistically positive or ignore legitimate concerns, but to replace harsh self-criticism with compassionate self-talk that motivates rather than paralyzes you.

Start by catching yourself in the act of negative self-talk and pausing to examine what you just thought. Ask yourself whether you would say those words to a good friend who was considering surgery, whether the thought is based on facts or fears, and whether believing this thought helps or hurts your ability to make good decisions for your health and happiness.

When you notice thoughts like "I always fail at everything," challenge them with specific evidence to the contrary. You haven't failed at everything, you've succeeded at many things in your life, and past weight loss attempts that didn't last don't predict future outcomes with a completely different approach. When you catch yourself thinking "I don't deserve to spend this money on myself," remind yourself that your health and happiness matter just as much as anyone else's, and that investing in your wellbeing benefits everyone who cares about you.

Replace "I'm taking the easy way out" with "I'm choosing an effective tool to help me succeed." Replace "I should be able to do this on my own" with "Using available resources to reach my goals is smart, not weak." Replace "What if I fail" with "What if I succeed beyond my wildest expectations." Replace "I can't afford this" with "I can't afford not to prioritize my health."

Create specific affirmations that counter your most persistent negative thoughts, but make sure they're believable and based on evidence rather than wishful thinking. Instead of "I'm perfect and nothing can go wrong," try "I'm capable of handling challenges and learning from setbacks." Instead of "Everyone will support my decision," try "I can handle other people's opinions without letting them derail my goals."

Practice self-compassion by treating yourself with the same kindness you would show a friend facing similar challenges. When you make a mistake or have a setback, respond with understanding rather than criticism. When you feel scared or uncertain, offer yourself comfort rather than judgment. When you need help or support, ask for it without shame or apology.

Develop a growth mindset about your ability to

change and learn new habits. Instead of viewing challenges as evidence that you're not cut out for success, see them as opportunities to develop skills and resilience. Instead of expecting perfection from day one, give yourself permission to learn as you go and improve over time.

Write down your new, more helpful thoughts and read them regularly until they become as automatic as the old negative patterns used to be. Record yourself saying encouraging things and play them back when you need to hear a supportive voice. Surround yourself with written reminders of your strength, your goals, and your reasons for choosing surgery.

Remember that changing thought patterns takes time and repetition, just like building any other new habit. You'll catch yourself falling back into old patterns of self-criticism, and that's normal and expected. The key is to notice when it happens and gently redirect your thoughts toward more helpful perspectives without criticizing yourself for having the negative thoughts in the first place.

The way you talk to yourself sets the tone for how you approach challenges, setbacks, and successes throughout your weight loss journey. Developing a kind, encouraging inner voice creates a foundation of confidence that can weather criticism from others, support you through difficult times, and help you maintain the motivation needed for long-term success.

Handling External Judgment Like a Boss

Other people's opinions about your decision to have weight loss surgery will range from supportive and encouraging to skeptical and judgmental, and you need strategies for handling all types of reactions without letting them affect your confidence or derail your plans. The key is understanding that most criticism comes from fear, misinformation, or the other person's own issues with weight and body image rather than legitimate concerns about your wellbeing.

When someone says "Have you tried just eating less and exercising more," respond with "Yes, I've tried many approaches over the years, and I'm choosing the one with the highest success rate for long-term weight loss." You don't owe anyone a detailed explanation of your diet history or a defense of your decision, but a brief, confident response shuts down further debate while asserting your right to make informed choices about your own body.

When people mention horror stories or complications they've heard about, say "Every surgery has risks, and I've discussed them thoroughly with my medical team. The risks of remaining at my current weight are actually higher than the risks of surgery." This acknowledges their concern without getting drawn into a debate about statistics or worst-case scenarios that may not even be accurate or current.

For comments about taking the easy way out, try "Surgery is a tool, not a magic solution. It still requires significant lifestyle changes and ongoing commitment to succeed." This corrects the misconception that surgery is effortless while demonstrating that you understand the work involved and are prepared to do it.

When family members or friends express worry about your safety, respond with "I appreciate your concern, and I want you to know that I've researched this thoroughly and chosen an experienced surgeon at an accredited facility. I'm confident in my decision and would love your support." This validates their feelings while establishing that your decision is final and asking for what you need from them.

For passive-aggressive comments about your appearance or eating habits after surgery, use phrases like "I'm happy with my progress and how I feel," or "My doctor and I are pleased with my results," or simply "Thank you for your concern." These responses don't engage with the underlying criticism but make it clear that you're not open to debate about your choices or outcomes.

When people ask intrusive questions about your weight loss, costs, or personal details, remember that you don't have to answer just because someone asks. "That's personal" or "I prefer not to discuss details" or "I'm focusing on my health and happiness" are all perfectly acceptable responses that maintain your privacy without being rude.

Set clear boundaries with people who repeatedly make negative comments or try to undermine your decision. "I've made my choice and I'm not open to further discussion about it" or "I need you to stop commenting on my weight and eating habits" or "If you can't be supportive, I'd prefer we talk about other topics" establishes limits on what you're willing to tolerate.

For people who seem threatened by your transformation or act differently toward you as you lose weight, address the issue directly but kindly. "I've noticed some tension between us lately, and I hope my weight loss isn't affecting our relationship. You're important to me and I want us to stay close" opens the door for honest conversation while reassuring them that you value the relationship.

Remember that you can't control other people's reactions, but you can control how you respond to them. Some people will surprise you with their support, others will disappoint you with their criticism, and most will adjust to your new lifestyle over time as they see that you're still the same person in a healthier body.

Practice your responses ahead of time so you're not caught off guard when criticism comes. Role-play difficult conversations with supportive friends or family members, write down your standard responses to common comments, and rehearse confident body language and tone of voice that matches your words.

The goal isn't to convince everyone that surgery is the right choice or to win arguments about weight loss methods. The goal is to protect your mental space, maintain your confidence, and surround yourself with people who support your health and happiness rather than undermine your efforts to improve your life.

Building Your Confidence Muscle

Confidence isn't something you either have or don't have, it's a skill you can develop through practice, and building unshakeable self-belief is crucial for navigating the challenges and changes that come with weight loss surgery. The stronger your confidence muscle becomes, the less power other people's criticism has over your mood, your decisions, and your progress toward your goals.

Start by documenting your strengths and past successes, not just related to weight loss but in all areas of your life. Write down challenges you've overcome, skills you've developed, goals you've achieved, and times when you've shown courage, persistence, or resilience. This evidence contradicts the inner critic's narrative that you're weak or incapable of success and reminds you of your track record of handling difficult situations.

Create a daily practice of acknowledging your efforts and progress, regardless of how small they might seem. Celebrate researching surgeons, attending information sessions, completing medical evaluations, asking questions, and taking any step toward your goals. Confidence builds through accumulated evidence that you can take action and follow through on commitments to yourself.

Develop competence in areas related to your surgery and recovery by learning about nutrition, meal planning, exercise options, and lifestyle changes that support long-term success. The more you know about what to expect and how to handle various situations, the more confident you'll feel about your ability to navigate the journey successfully.

Practice assertiveness in low-stakes situations so you're prepared to advocate for yourself when it matters most. This might mean asking for what you need at restaurants, expressing your preferences in social situations, or setting small boundaries with family and friends. Each time you speak up for yourself, you strengthen your confidence in your ability to handle bigger challenges.

Surround yourself with evidence of your worth and capabilities by keeping a success journal, displaying photos from happy moments in your life, saving encouraging messages from supportive people, and creating visual reminders of your goals and motivations. When criticism threatens to undermine your confidence, you have concrete evidence to counter those negative messages.

Challenge yourself to try new things and step outside your comfort zone in small ways, building proof that you can handle uncertainty and adapt to new situations. This might mean trying a new restaurant, attending a social event you would normally avoid, or participating in an activity that feels slightly intimidating. Each success expands your confidence in your ability to handle change and growth.

Develop a pre-surgery routine that makes you feel strong and capable, whether that's exercising regularly, practicing meditation, reading inspiring books, or engaging in hobbies that showcase your skills and talents. Having activities that consistently boost your mood and confidence creates a foundation of positive self-regard that criticism can't easily shake.

Practice positive self-talk and visualization, imagining yourself successfully navigating challenging situations with grace and confidence. Mental rehearsal helps you feel more prepared for real-life scenarios and builds neural pathways associated with successful outcomes rather than fearful predictions.

Connect with other people who have had weight loss surgery and achieved the kind of results you want, either through support groups, online communities, or personal relationships. Seeing examples of success that look like your situation builds confidence in your own ability to achieve similar outcomes.

Invest in your appearance and self-care in ways that make you feel good about yourself right now, not just after you lose weight. This might mean getting a haircut you love, buying clothes that fit well in your current size, taking care of your skin, or engaging in activities that make you feel attractive and confident in your own body.

Remember that confidence isn't about feeling fearless

or never having doubts. It's about trusting yourself to handle whatever comes up, learning from setbacks without letting them define you, and maintaining belief in your ability to create positive change in your life even when the path isn't smooth or predictable.

The confidence you build now becomes the foundation for everything that comes later in your journey. It helps you recover from surgery with a positive attitude, navigate the challenges of changing eating habits with patience and self-compassion, handle other people's reactions with grace and boundaries, and maintain your progress over the long term because you believe you deserve success.

Chapter 2 Make Your Move

These exercises help you identify negative thought patterns, develop more supportive self-talk, prepare responses to criticism, and build daily habits that strengthen your confidence and resilience throughout your weight loss surgery journey.

Begin with a thought audit by carrying a small notebook or using your phone to track negative thoughts about yourself, your decision, or your likelihood of success for one full week. Write down each critical thought as it occurs, noting what triggered it and how it made you feel. At the end of the week, review your notes to identify the most common patterns and themes in your self-criticism.

Create replacement thoughts for your most frequent negative patterns by writing more balanced, helpful alternatives to each critical thought you identified. Make sure these new thoughts are believable and based on evidence rather than empty positive thinking. Practice your replacement thoughts by reading them aloud daily until they start to feel as automatic as the old negative patterns.

Develop your criticism response script by writing down specific responses to common negative comments about weight loss surgery. Include responses for "have you tried just dieting," "surgery is dangerous," "you're taking the easy way out," "you look fine the way you are," and any other comments you expect to encounter. Practice these responses until you can deliver them confidently and calmly.

Build your evidence file by creating a written list of your strengths, past successes, challenges you've overcome, and positive qualities that have nothing to do with your weight. Include specific examples and details that demonstrate your capability, resilience, and worth. Add to this file regularly and review it whenever you need a confidence boost.

Establish confidence-building daily rituals that make you feel strong, capable, and worthy of success. This might include morning affirmations, evening gratitude practices, exercise routines, creative activities, or self-care habits that consistently boost your mood and self-regard. Commit to at least one confidence-building activity every day.

Practice boundary setting by identifying people in your life who might be critical or unsupportive of your surgery decision and planning specific strategies for limiting their influence on your mental state. This might include reducing contact during vulnerable times, changing the subject when they bring up your weight, or directly asking them to stop commenting on your choices.

Create a support network map by listing people who are genuinely supportive of your health and happiness, including friends, family members, healthcare providers, online communities, or support groups. Make a plan for staying connected with these positive influences and reaching out to them when you need encouragement or reassurance.

Finally, write a confidence letter to yourself describing all the reasons you're capable of succeeding with weight loss surgery, including your motivations, your preparation, your support system, and your track record of overcoming challenges. Date this letter and read it whenever doubt creeps in or criticism threatens to undermine your resolve.

Review and practice these tools regularly, especially during the weeks leading up to your surgery when anxiety and outside opinions might feel more overwhelming. The mental preparation you do now creates a foundation of confidence and resilience that will serve you throughout your entire transformation journey.

Chapter 3: The Emotional Earthquake

Weight loss surgery doesn't just change your stomach, it shakes up every single part of your life in ways nobody warns you about. You walk into the hospital thinking about smaller clothes and better health, but you walk out into a world where everything from family dinners to work lunches to your own reflection in the mirror feels different and sometimes overwhelming. This isn't just about learning new eating habits or taking vitamins.

Surgery triggers what feels like an emotional earthquake that affects your relationships, your identity, your coping mechanisms, your social life, your self-image, and every single way you've been navigating the world up until now. The physical changes happen fast, but the emotional adjustments take much longer and require tools most people don't think to develop ahead of time.

You might find yourself grieving the loss of food as your primary comfort, feeling anxious about eating in public when you can only take a few bites, struggling with compliments because you don't know how to accept praise about your appearance, or dealing with friends and family members who act differently toward you as your body changes. These reactions catch most people off guard because they're focused on the excitement of losing weight rather than preparing for the emotional complexity of transformation.

The people who succeed long-term don't just prepare their bodies for surgery, they prepare their hearts and minds for everything that comes after. They build emotional tools before they need them, practice new coping skills while they're still learning new eating habits, and create support systems that can handle the ups and downs of such a dramatic life change.

Why Surgery Shakes Everything Up

Your relationship with food has been developing for decades, and it's connected to everything else in your life in ways you might not fully realize until surgery forces you to change those patterns. Food has probably been your comfort when you're stressed, your reward when you accomplish something, your entertainment when you're bored, your companion when you're lonely, and your way of participating in celebrations, family gatherings, work events, and social situations.

When surgery dramatically limits how much you can

eat and changes what foods you can tolerate, you lose all of those emotional functions at once, and your brain scrambles to figure out new ways to handle stress, boredom, sadness, anxiety, celebration, and social connection.

The physical restriction happens immediately after surgery, but developing new emotional coping strategies takes months or even years, creating a gap between losing your old comfort mechanisms and building reliable new ones. During this transition period, you might feel more emotionally vulnerable than usual, more sensitive to criticism or stress, more likely to feel overwhelmed by situations that used to be manageable when you could eat your way through them.

Your identity shifts in ways that feel both exciting and unsettling as you lose weight and start getting different reactions from people around you. You might have thought of yourself as the funny one who uses humor to deflect attention from your weight, or the caretaker who focuses on everyone else's needs to avoid dealing with your own body image issues, or the reliable friend who always brings the best food to gatherings.

As your body changes, these roles might not fit anymore, and you have to figure out who you are when you're not hiding behind your weight or defining yourself by your size. The attention that comes with dramatic weight loss can feel wonderful and terrible at the same time. You might love fitting into smaller clothes and getting compliments, but feel uncomfortable with strangers commenting on your body or coworkers asking personal questions about your eating habits. You might enjoy feeling more confident and attractive, but struggle with guilt about caring how you look or worry that people only like you now because you're thinner.

Your relationships change because weight loss affects the dynamic between you and everyone in your life, from your spouse who might feel threatened by your new confidence to your friends who might feel judged by your healthy choices to your family members who might miss the old you who participated fully in food-centered activities. Some relationships grow stronger as people support your transformation, others become strained as people adjust to your new lifestyle, and some reveal themselves to be based on keeping you small rather than celebrating your growth.

The speed of change after surgery can feel overwhelming because you're adjusting to a new body, new eating habits, new energy levels, new clothes, new social situations, and new reactions from other people all at the same time. Your brain needs time to catch up with your body, and your emotions need time to process such a dramatic shift in how you move through the world.

Understanding that these emotional challenges are normal and temporary helps you prepare for them instead of being blindsided by feelings you didn't expect. The earthquake is real, but it's also the process of your old life cracking open to make room for the new life you're building, and having the right tools makes all the difference in how you navigate the shaking.

Surgery gives you a powerful tool for weight loss, but emotional preparation gives you the resilience to use that tool effectively for the rest of your life. The physical changes are just the beginning of a transformation that touches every aspect of who you are and how you live, and preparing for that reality helps you embrace the process instead of being overwhelmed by it.

Grieving Your Old Life

Nobody talks about the grief that comes with weight loss surgery, but it's real and it's necessary and it catches most people completely off guard when it hits them a few weeks or months after their procedure. You expected to feel happy about losing weight and getting healthier, but you didn't expect to feel sad about losing parts of your old life that brought you comfort, even if those same parts were also holding you back from your goals.

Grief shows up when you realize you can't eat birthday cake at your daughter's party without getting sick, when you have to leave food on your plate at your favorite restaurant because three bites fill you up completely, when you can't drink wine with your friends during girls' night because alcohol makes you feel awful, when you have to pack your own snacks for road trips because gas station food doesn't work with your new eating plan.

These losses feel silly to mourn because they're connected to the exact behaviors that kept you overweight and unhappy, but grief doesn't care about logic. You're mourning the loss of food as your reliable friend, the one thing that was always available when you needed comfort, celebration, distraction, or reward. You're grieving the simplicity of your old life when you could eat whatever you wanted without planning, measuring, or worrying about protein content and vitamin absorption. You're missing the version of yourself who could blend into crowds, avoid attention, and use your weight as an excuse to stay in your comfort zone.

The grief might show up as sadness when you watch other people eat foods you used to love, anger when you feel restricted by your new eating requirements, anxiety about navigating social situations that revolve around food, or guilt about missing aspects of your old life when you know the surgery was the right choice for your health and happiness.

Some people feel guilty about grieving because they think they should only feel grateful for the opportunity to lose weight and improve their health. They worry that missing their old eating habits means they're not committed to their new lifestyle or that they made the wrong decision about surgery. This guilt makes the grief worse because you're not allowing yourself to process the natural sadness that comes with any major life transition.

Grief is not a sign that you regret your decision or that you're not grateful for your surgery results. It's a normal response to losing familiar coping mechanisms, changing long-established habits, and adjusting to a completely different way of living in your body and moving through the world. Every major positive change involves some loss, and acknowledging that loss doesn't diminish the benefits of the change.

The grieving process looks different for everyone, but

it usually includes stages of denial, anger, bargaining, depression, and acceptance that don't happen in a neat order or timeline. You might find yourself trying to eat the way you used to and getting sick, feeling angry about your food restrictions when everyone around you can eat normally, wishing you could have just a little bit more flexibility with your eating plan, feeling sad about how much your life has changed, and eventually accepting your new relationship with food as part of your healthier lifestyle.

Allow yourself to feel whatever comes up without judgment or attempts to rush through the process. Talk to other people who have had surgery and understand the emotional complexity of this journey. Write about your feelings, cry when you need to, and give yourself permission to miss aspects of your old life while still being committed to your new one.

Create new rituals and traditions that don't revolve around food to replace some of what you're losing. Instead of bonding with friends over big meals, suggest activities like walking, shopping, or going to movies. Instead of celebrating achievements with food, treat yourself to new clothes, spa services, or experiences you couldn't enjoy at your previous weight.

Remember that grief has an end point, even though it

doesn't feel that way when you're in the middle of it. Most people find that the sadness about their food restrictions fades as they discover new foods they enjoy, develop confidence in navigating social situations, and experience the benefits of their healthier lifestyle. The identity confusion settles as you figure out who you are in your new body and build relationships based on more than shared eating habits.

The grief you feel now is making space for the joy that comes with living in a body that feels good, having energy for activities you love, wearing clothes that make you feel confident, and participating fully in life instead of watching from the sidelines. Honoring the loss makes room for appreciating the gains, and both emotions can coexist as you adjust to your transformed life.

Managing Pre-Surgery Anxiety

The weeks leading up to your surgery date bring a unique type of anxiety that combines excitement about finally taking action with terror about everything that could go wrong, and learning to manage these intense emotions helps you approach your surgery with confidence instead of panic. The anxiety feels overwhelming because you're facing something completely unknown while making an irreversible decision that will affect every aspect of your life going forward.

Your mind cycles through worst-case scenarios, from surgical complications to regaining all the weight to ruining your relationships to never being able to enjoy food again, and each fear feels equally possible and equally catastrophic when anxiety is running the show.

The pre-surgery diet phase often intensifies anxiety because you're already changing your eating habits, dealing with hunger and cravings, and getting a preview of how different your relationship with food will become after surgery. You might feel cranky, tired, and emotionally vulnerable while trying to follow strict dietary guidelines, complete medical evaluations, and handle other people's reactions to your upcoming surgery.

Physical symptoms of anxiety like trouble sleeping, changes in appetite, difficulty concentrating, muscle tension, headaches, or stomach problems can make you feel worse and worry that you're not mentally ready for such a big step. The irony is that feeling anxious about surgery doesn't mean you're not ready for it, it means you understand the significance of what you're about to do and you're having a normal human response to major change.

Start managing pre-surgery anxiety by distinguishing

between productive worry and unproductive spiraling. Productive worry leads to helpful actions like researching your surgeon, preparing your home for recovery, arranging help during your healing process, and learning about post-surgery nutrition requirements. Unproductive worry involves repeatedly imagining disasters you can't control, reading horror stories online, or trying to predict and prevent every possible negative outcome.

When you catch yourself spiraling into catastrophic thinking, use grounding techniques to bring your attention back to the present moment instead of getting lost in fearful predictions about the future. Focus on your breathing, name five things you can see around you, listen to calming music, take a warm shower, or engage in any activity that helps you feel connected to your body and your immediate environment rather than your racing thoughts.

Create a realistic picture of what to expect by talking to your surgical team about the actual risks, recovery timeline, and common experiences rather than relying on internet research or secondhand stories from people who may not have accurate information. Ask specific questions about pain management, dietary progression, activity restrictions, and warning signs to watch for during recovery so you feel prepared instead of blindsided by normal post-surgery experiences.

Develop a pre-surgery routine that includes activities that make you feel calm, confident, and connected to your reasons for choosing surgery. This might include daily walks, meditation or prayer, journaling about your goals and motivations, talking to supportive friends or family members, or engaging in hobbies that help you feel like yourself rather than just a person preparing for surgery.

Limit your exposure to negative information and unsupportive people during the weeks leading up to surgery when your emotional defenses are lower than usual. Stop reading online forums that focus on complications and problems, avoid people who want to debate your decision, and create boundaries around discussions of your surgery with anyone who isn't genuinely supportive of your choice.

Practice relaxation techniques like deep breathing, progressive muscle relaxation, guided imagery, or meditation that you can use before, during, and after surgery to manage anxiety and promote healing. Learning these skills ahead of time makes them more effective when you actually need them, and having concrete tools for managing anxiety gives you more confidence in your ability to handle whatever comes up.

Focus on the things you can control rather than

worrying about variables that are outside your influence. You can't control whether you'll have complications, but you can choose an experienced surgeon and follow all pre-surgery instructions carefully. You can't control how quickly you'll lose weight, but you can commit to following your post-surgery eating plan and staying active as recommended.

Remember that some anxiety is actually helpful because it motivates you to prepare thoroughly, ask important questions, and take your surgery seriously rather than approaching it casually. The goal isn't to eliminate all nervousness, but to keep anxiety at a manageable level that doesn't interfere with your sleep, your relationships, or your ability to take care of yourself during this important time.

Talk to your healthcare team if anxiety becomes overwhelming or starts interfering with your daily functioning, because they can provide additional resources, adjust medications if necessary, or help you develop more effective coping strategies. Taking care of your mental health is just as important as taking care of your physical health as you prepare for surgery.

Creating Your Emotional Toolkit

Building a collection of healthy coping strategies

before surgery gives you alternatives to food when you're dealing with stress, sadness, boredom, anxiety, anger, or any other emotion that used to trigger eating episodes. Your toolkit needs to include quick fixes for immediate emotional relief, longer-term strategies for ongoing stress management, and emergency plans for handling intense emotions without turning to old patterns that no longer serve your goals.

Start by identifying your emotional eating triggers so you know which situations and feelings require the most preparation and support. Common triggers include work stress, relationship conflicts, financial worries, family drama, loneliness, boredom, celebration, disappointment, anger, sadness, and anxiety, but your personal list might include specific situations like driving long distances, watching television at night, or dealing with difficult people in your life.

For each trigger you identify, develop at least three alternative responses that provide comfort, distraction, or stress relief without involving food.

When you're stressed, your alternatives might include taking a hot bath, calling a supportive friend, going for a walk, listening to music, doing deep breathing exercises, writing in a journal, or engaging in a hobby that requires concentration and provides a sense of accomplishment. When you're sad, you might try watching a funny movie, looking at photos that make you smile, spending time with pets, doing something kind for someone else, or allowing yourself to cry while practicing self-compassion.

When you're bored, replace mindless eating with activities that engage your hands and mind like puzzles, crafts, reading, organizing spaces in your home, learning something new online, or calling someone you haven't talked to in a while. When you're celebrating, create new traditions around experiences rather than food, like buying yourself flowers, taking photos to commemorate the moment, sharing your good news with people who care about you, or doing something special that aligns with your health goals.

Build physical comfort strategies that provide the soothing sensation you used to get from eating without the food component. This might include using a heating pad, taking warm baths, getting massages, using soft blankets, cuddling with pets, or creating a cozy environment with candles, comfortable lighting, and relaxing scents.

Develop social connection tools for times when loneliness or isolation used to trigger eating episodes. Create a list of people you can call or text when you need support, join online communities related to your interests or your surgery journey, schedule regular activities with friends and family members, volunteer for causes you care about, or find ways to be around other people even when you don't feel like socializing.

Practice mindfulness techniques that help you sit with uncomfortable emotions instead of immediately trying to make them go away with food. Learn to notice when emotions arise, name them without judgment, breathe through the physical sensations they create in your body, and remind yourself that all feelings are temporary and manageable without being fed.

Create movement-based coping strategies that use physical activity to process emotions and release tension. This doesn't have to mean intense exercise, it can include gentle stretching, dancing to music you love, walking around your neighborhood, doing yard work, cleaning or organizing your home, or any activity that gets your body moving and your mind focused on something other than eating.

Build creative outlets that provide emotional expression and stress relief while giving you a sense of accomplishment and purpose. This might include writing, drawing, painting, crafts, music, photography, gardening, cooking healthy meals for your family, or any activity that allows you to create something meaningful while processing your emotions.

Develop spiritual or philosophical practices that help you find meaning and perspective during difficult times. This might include prayer, meditation, reading inspirational books, spending time in nature, practicing gratitude, volunteering, or engaging with whatever belief system provides you with comfort and guidance.

Create an emergency plan for handling intense emotional crises when you feel overwhelmed and at risk of turning to old eating patterns for comfort. This plan should include specific people to call, immediate actions to take, reminders of your goals and motivations, and professional resources like counselors or support groups that can provide additional help when needed.

Practice using your new coping strategies regularly, even when you don't feel particularly stressed or emotional, so they become familiar and automatic rather than foreign and awkward when you actually need them. The more you use these tools in low-stakes situations, the more likely you are to remember and trust them during high-stakes emotional moments.

Remember that building new coping skills takes time

and practice, and you'll probably still feel tempted to use food for comfort sometimes, especially during the first few months after surgery. Having multiple options in your toolkit means you can try different strategies until you find what works best for different situations and emotional states.

Chapter 3 Make Your Move

These exercises help you prepare emotionally for the changes that come with weight loss surgery by identifying potential challenges, building coping skills, creating support systems, and developing the resilience needed to navigate your transformation successfully.

Complete an emotional eating assessment by tracking your eating patterns and emotional states for one full week before surgery. Note what you eat, when you eat it, how hungry you actually were, what emotions you were feeling, and what situations or thoughts triggered the desire to eat. This baseline helps you identify your most common emotional eating triggers and the feelings you'll need alternative coping strategies for after surgery.

Create your personalized emotional toolkit by listing at least five healthy coping strategies for each of your most common emotional triggers. Include quick options that take less than five minutes, medium options that take fifteen to thirty minutes, and longer activities that provide deeper emotional processing and stress relief. Test each strategy at least once before surgery to make sure it actually helps you feel better.

Write a grief acknowledgment letter to yourself recognizing what you'll miss about your old relationship with food and your pre-surgery lifestyle. Include specific foods, eating experiences, social situations, and aspects of your identity that will change after surgery. End the letter by acknowledging that grief is normal and temporary, and that making space for sadness also makes space for the joy that comes with achieving your health goals.

Develop your anxiety management plan by identifying your specific pre-surgery worries and creating concrete actions for addressing each concern. Include relaxation techniques you'll practice daily, questions you want to ask your surgical team, preparations you can make for recovery, and people you can talk to when anxiety feels overwhelming. Practice your chosen relaxation techniques daily so they become automatic responses to stress.

Build your support network map by identifying people who can provide different types of help during your surgery and recovery period. Include practical support like meal preparation and transportation, emotional support like listening and encouragement, informational support like advice from others who have had surgery, and professional support like counselors or support groups. Contact these people before surgery to arrange specific help and set expectations.

Create post-surgery social situation strategies by thinking through upcoming events, holidays, and regular activities that involve food and planning how you'll handle them with your new eating requirements. Include what you'll eat, how you'll explain your small portions, ways to participate in celebrations that don't revolve around food, and responses to questions or comments about your eating habits.

Design your identity exploration exercises by writing about who you are beyond your weight, what qualities and interests define you that have nothing to do with your size, and who you want to become as you lose weight and gain confidence. Include values that guide your decisions, goals that excite you, and relationships that matter most to you. Review this regularly as your body changes to stay connected to your authentic self.

Finally, establish your emotional check-in routine by scheduling weekly times to assess your emotional state, review your coping strategies, celebrate your progress, and adjust your approach based on what's working and what needs improvement. Include questions about your mood, stress levels, relationship satisfaction, and overall life satisfaction to track your emotional wellbeing alongside your physical transformation.

Practice these tools consistently during your pre-surgery preparation period so they become familiar and reliable resources when you need them most. The emotional preparation you do now creates a foundation of resilience that supports your success throughout your entire weight loss journey and beyond.

Chapter 4: Relationship Survival Guide

Your weight loss surgery doesn't just change your body, it changes every single relationship in your life, and most people aren't prepared for how complicated this gets. You think everyone will be happy for you when you start losing weight and getting healthier, but the reality is much more complex and sometimes painful than you expect.

Some people will surprise you with their support and encouragement. Others will shock you with their criticism, jealousy, or attempts to sabotage your progress in ways that feel like betrayal from people you trusted most. Your spouse might feel threatened by your new confidence and the attention you're getting from strangers. Your best friend might start making passive-aggressive comments about how you think you're better than everyone now. Your mother might keep bringing your favorite desserts to family gatherings even after you've explained that you can't eat sugar anymore.

The people closest to you have gotten used to a certain version of you, and when that version starts changing dramatically, it affects the balance of your relationships in ways nobody talks about during surgery preparation. Your transformation forces everyone around you to examine their own choices about health, weight, and self-care, and not everyone is ready for that kind of self-reflection.

Learning to protect your progress while maintaining important relationships requires skills most people don't develop until they're already dealing with relationship drama that threatens to derail their success. The key is understanding why people react the way they do, recognizing sabotage before it damages your confidence, setting boundaries that protect your mental health, and building a support system of people who genuinely celebrate your transformation instead of feeling threatened by it.

When Loved Ones Don't Love Your Decision

The resistance from family and friends often catches people completely off guard because it comes from people who claim to love you and want you to be happy and healthy. You expect strangers to have opinions about your surgery, but you don't expect your sister to tell you you're taking the easy way out, or your husband to worry that you'll leave him when you get thin, or your best friend to start acting weird every time you decline food at restaurants.

This resistance usually stems from fear rather than genuine concern for your wellbeing, even though it gets expressed as worry about your safety or criticism of your choices.

Your spouse might fear that your increased confidence will make you realize you deserve better treatment, or that other people will find you attractive and threaten your relationship, or that you'll become a different person who no longer wants the same lifestyle you've been sharing. These fears feel real and threatening even when they're based on insecurities rather than evidence, and they often get expressed as criticism of your decision to have surgery.

Your parents might resist your surgery because they feel guilty about your childhood eating patterns, family food traditions, or genetic factors that contributed to your weight struggles. They might interpret your decision to have surgery as criticism of how they raised you or fed you, leading them to defend their choices by attacking yours. They might also fear losing the caregiving role they've played in your life or worry that your success will highlight their own struggles with weight and health.

Your friends might feel threatened by your

transformation because it forces them to examine their own choices about health and self-care. When you start losing weight and gaining confidence, it becomes harder for them to make excuses about their own situations, and instead of feeling inspired by your success, they might feel judged or left behind. Friends who bonded with you over shared complaints about weight, dating, or body image might not know how to relate to you when those shared struggles are no longer part of your identity.

Your siblings might compete with you for attention, approval, or the role of family success story, leading them to minimize your achievements or point out potential problems with your approach. If you've always been the heavy one in the family, your weight loss might shift family dynamics in ways that feel uncomfortable for everyone, especially if other family members also struggle with weight and aren't ready to address their own health issues.

Coworkers might feel uncomfortable with your dramatic transformation because it changes the social dynamics at work and forces them to acknowledge that significant change is possible, which can feel threatening if they've been making excuses about their own situations. They might also feel awkward about commenting on your appearance or unsure how to interact with the new, more confident version of you.

Understanding that resistance comes from other people's fears and insecurities rather than legitimate concerns about your wellbeing helps you respond with compassion instead of anger, but it doesn't mean you have to tolerate behavior that undermines your success or damages your confidence. You can acknowledge their fears while still protecting your progress and maintaining your boundaries.

When someone expresses concern about your surgery, listen to understand whether they're sharing genuine worry or expressing their own discomfort with your changes. Genuine concern focuses on your safety and happiness, while fear-based resistance focuses on how your changes affect them or challenges their own choices. Respond to genuine concern with information and reassurance, but don't waste energy trying to convince people who are really expressing their own insecurities.

Remember that you can't control other people's reactions to your transformation, but you can control how much influence you allow those reactions to have on your confidence, your choices, and your progress toward your goals. Some relationships will grow stronger as people adjust to your new lifestyle and see how much happier and healthier you become. Others might need time and space to process their own feelings before they can be genuinely supportive. A few might reveal themselves to be based on keeping you small rather than celebrating your growth, and those relationships might need to be limited or ended entirely.

The people who truly love you will eventually come around to supporting your transformation, even if they need time to work through their initial fears and concerns. The people who continue to undermine your success after you've explained how important this journey is to you are showing you that their comfort matters more to them than your health and happiness, and that information helps you make informed decisions about how much energy to invest in those relationships.

Spotting Sabotage Before It Derails You

Sabotage doesn't always look like someone actively trying to make you fail, and the most dangerous forms of undermining behavior come from people who claim to love and support you while consistently acting in ways that make your success more difficult. Learning to recognize these patterns early helps you address them before they damage your progress or your confidence.

Food sabotage is the most obvious form and includes people who keep offering you foods you can't eat, bringing your old favorites to gatherings after you've explained your dietary restrictions, suggesting restaurants that don't have options that work for your eating plan, or making comments about how you're being too restrictive or obsessive about your food choices.

This behavior often gets disguised as caring or hospitality, with comments like "one bite won't hurt you" or "you're getting too thin, you need to eat more" or "I made this especially for you" when they know perfectly well that you can't eat whatever they're offering.

Emotional sabotage involves people who consistently undermine your confidence, minimize your achievements, or create drama and stress that triggers your old coping patterns. This might include making comments about how you think you're better than everyone now that you're losing weight, pointing out every time you struggle or make a mistake, comparing your progress to other people's results, or creating conflict during times when you're already feeling vulnerable or stressed.

Social sabotage includes people who exclude you

from activities because of your new eating requirements, make you feel guilty for not participating in food-centered events the way you used to, schedule gatherings at places or times that make it difficult for you to stick to your eating plan, or consistently choose activities that revolve around foods you can't eat instead of finding alternatives that work for everyone.

Identity sabotage involves people who refuse to acknowledge your transformation or treat you like the same person you were before surgery, even when your body, confidence, and lifestyle have changed dramatically. This might include continuing to make jokes about your weight, buying you clothes in your old size, referring to you as "the big one" in family photos, or dismissing your new interests and activities as phases you'll get over.

Relationship sabotage comes from partners who feel threatened by your transformation and try to undermine your confidence or progress to keep you dependent on them. This might include criticizing your appearance even when you're getting compliments from others, discouraging you from social activities where you might meet new people, making negative comments about how surgery has changed you, or withdrawing affection and support when you're feeling vulnerable about your changing body.

The key to spotting sabotage is paying attention to patterns rather than isolated incidents, because most saboteurs don't set out to deliberately harm your progress. They act out of their own fears, insecurities, and discomfort with change, but the impact on your success is the same regardless of their intentions.

Notice when someone consistently makes choices that make your journey more difficult, even after you've explained what you need from them. Notice when their support feels conditional on you staying small, unsuccessful, or dependent on them. Notice when their comments about your progress focus on potential problems rather than celebrating your achievements. Notice when they create stress or drama during times when you're already struggling with other challenges.

Trust your instincts when something feels off about someone's reaction to your transformation, even if you can't immediately identify what's wrong or they're not doing anything overtly harmful. Your gut feelings about people's motivations are usually accurate, and learning to trust those instincts helps you protect yourself from subtle forms of undermining behavior that might not be obvious to outside observers.

Document patterns of sabotaging behavior by keeping

notes about specific incidents, comments, or actions that make you feel unsupported or undermined. This helps you see patterns more clearly and gives you concrete examples to reference when you need to address the behavior directly or explain your concerns to other people.

Remember that calling out sabotage doesn't require proof of malicious intent, because the impact on your progress matters more than the other person's motivations. You have the right to ask people to change behaviors that make your success more difficult, regardless of whether they're doing it on purpose or unconsciously acting out their own issues.

Address sabotage directly but calmly, focusing on specific behaviors and their impact on your goals rather than making accusations about the person's character or intentions. Use phrases like "when you bring dessert to dinner after I've explained that I can't eat sugar, it makes it harder for me to stick to my eating plan" rather than "you're trying to sabotage my diet" because the first approach focuses on changeable behavior while the second creates defensiveness and conflict.

Set clear consequences for continued sabotaging behavior, and be prepared to follow through on them if the person doesn't change their actions after you've addressed the issue directly. This might mean limiting contact with people who consistently undermine your progress, declining invitations to events where you can't count on support, or ending relationships that are based on keeping you unsuccessful rather than celebrating your growth.

Setting Boundaries That Stick

Boundaries aren't walls that keep people out of your life, they're guidelines that protect your mental health, your progress, and your ability to maintain the lifestyle changes that surgery requires. Most people struggle with boundaries because they confuse being kind with being permissive, but the kindest thing you can do for yourself and your relationships is to be clear about what behavior you will and won't accept from others.

Start by identifying the specific behaviors that interfere with your success or make you feel unsupported, criticized, or undermined in your weight loss journey. This might include people commenting on your food choices, asking personal questions about your weight loss or surgery details, offering you foods you can't eat after you've declined, making jokes about your appearance or eating habits, comparing your progress to other people's results, or creating guilt about your new lifestyle choices. Each behavior that consistently makes you feel worse about yourself or your progress needs a clear boundary.

Communicate your boundaries clearly and specifically rather than hoping people will figure out what you need through hints or passive-aggressive comments. Use direct language like "I need you to stop commenting on how much I'm eating at meals" or "I'm not comfortable discussing the details of my surgery with coworkers" or "I need you to respect my food choices without trying to convince me to eat differently" rather than vague requests like "please be more supportive" that leave too much room for interpretation.

Explain the consequence that will happen if the boundary is crossed, and make sure it's something you're actually willing and able to follow through on rather than an empty threat that undermines your credibility. This might mean "If you continue to bring desserts to family dinners after I've asked you not to, I'll eat before I come and won't participate in the meal portion of the gathering" or "If you keep making comments about my appearance, I'll need to limit our conversations to topics that don't involve my body or my weight loss."

Follow through consistently when boundaries are crossed, even if it feels uncomfortable or creates temporary conflict in the relationship. People learn to respect your boundaries when they see that you're serious about enforcing them, but they learn to ignore your boundaries when you make exceptions or fail to implement the consequences you've stated. Consistency is more important than perfection, and following through most of the time is better than never following through at all.

Practice boundary-setting in low-stakes situations so you build confidence in your ability to advocate for yourself when it really matters. This might mean declining social invitations when you need time to rest, asking people not to comment on your appearance, or requesting that family gatherings include food options that work with your eating plan. Each time you successfully set and maintain a small boundary, you build trust in your ability to handle bigger challenges.

Remember that other people's reactions to your boundaries give you valuable information about their character and their investment in your wellbeing. People who genuinely care about you will respect your boundaries even if they don't fully understand them, because they prioritize your comfort and success over their own convenience or preferences. People who react with anger, guilt-tripping, or boundary-testing are showing you that their needs matter more to them than yours.

Expect some pushback when you start setting boundaries, especially from people who have benefited from your previous lack of limits. They might accuse you of being selfish, oversensitive, or changed by your weight loss, but these reactions usually indicate that your boundaries are necessary and appropriate rather than evidence that you're being unreasonable.

Adjust your boundaries as needed based on your changing needs and circumstances, but don't abandon them entirely when they feel difficult to maintain. You might need stricter boundaries during the first few months after surgery when you're still learning new eating habits and feeling emotionally vulnerable, and you might be able to relax some limits as you become more confident in your ability to handle challenging situations.

Create different types of boundaries for different relationships and situations, recognizing that you might need firmer limits with some people than others based on their history of supportive or undermining behavior. Your boundaries with a consistently supportive friend might be much more flexible than your boundaries with a family member who has a history of making critical comments about your weight and food choices.

Use boundaries to protect your time and energy as well as your emotional wellbeing, because transformation requires significant mental and physical resources that you can't afford to waste on managing other people's reactions to your changes. This might mean limiting time with people who drain your energy, declining invitations to events that create stress or temptation, or asking people to schedule conversations about your surgery at times when you feel prepared to handle their questions or concerns.

Remember that boundaries are ultimately about self-respect and self-care rather than controlling other people's behavior. You can't force anyone to treat you the way you want to be treated, but you can control your own responses and limit your exposure to behavior that interferes with your goals and your happiness.

Building Your Cheerleader Squad

Creating a strong support system of people who genuinely celebrate your transformation and encourage your success is just as important as identifying and limiting contact with people who undermine your progress. Your cheerleader squad doesn't have to be large, but it needs to include people who understand your goals, respect your choices, and consistently act in ways that support your health and happiness.

Look for people who ask how they can help rather than telling you what you should do differently, who celebrate your victories without minimizing them or comparing them to other people's achievements, who respect your food choices without trying to convince you to eat differently, and who treat your surgery as a positive tool for improving your health rather than a sign of weakness or failure.

Your support system might include family members who educate themselves about weight loss surgery and adjust family traditions to accommodate your new eating requirements, friends who suggest non-food activities for socializing and celebrate your progress without making it about appearance, coworkers who respect your privacy while offering practical support like bringing healthy options to work events, and healthcare providers who treat you as a whole person rather than just a surgical patient.

Consider joining support groups specifically for people who have had weight loss surgery, either in person or online, because these communities understand the unique challenges and experiences that come with this transformation in ways that people who haven't had surgery simply can't relate to. These groups provide practical advice, emotional support, and encouragement from people who have faced similar struggles and achieved similar goals.

Build relationships with people who inspire you to maintain healthy habits rather than people who enable old patterns or make excuses for unhealthy choices. This might mean spending more time with friends who enjoy physical activities, people who prioritize their health and wellbeing, or individuals who have successfully maintained significant lifestyle changes in their own lives.

Communicate clearly with your support people about what kind of help you need and when you need it, because even the most well-intentioned people can't read your mind or automatically know how to best support your journey. Let them know whether you want practical help like meal preparation or transportation, emotional support like listening and encouragement, or informational support like advice and resources.

Express appreciation regularly for the people who support your transformation, because maintaining supportive relationships requires effort from both sides and people need to know that their encouragement and help are valued and effective. Thank people specifically for actions that made a difference in your day or your progress, and let them know how their support contributes to your success.

Be willing to reciprocate support when your cheerleaders face their own challenges, because healthy relationships involve give and take rather than one person always receiving help while the other always provides it. This doesn't mean you have to solve everyone's problems, but it does mean showing up with the same kind of care and encouragement that you appreciate receiving from them.

Expand your support network gradually as you meet new people who align with your values and lifestyle, because transformation often involves outgrowing some relationships while building new ones that better match who you're becoming. Stay open to friendships with people who share your interests in health, fitness, personal growth, or other activities that support your new lifestyle.

Include professional support in your cheerleader squad when needed, such as counselors who specialize in weight loss surgery, nutritionists who understand your eating requirements, personal trainers who work with post-surgery clients, or medical professionals who monitor your health and progress. Professional support provides expertise and objectivity that friends and family members can't always offer.

Create different layers of support for different types of

needs, recognizing that no single person can meet all of your support requirements and that different people might be better at providing different kinds of help. You might have one friend who's great for workout motivation, another who's excellent for emotional support, and a family member who provides practical help with meal preparation or childcare.

Set boundaries with your support people as well, because even positive relationships need limits to remain healthy and sustainable. Let people know when you need space to process your own feelings, when you're not ready for advice, or when you need them to listen without trying to fix your problems. Good support people will respect these boundaries and adjust their approach based on what you actually need rather than what they think you should need.

Remember that building a strong support system takes time and effort, and you might need to try several different groups, activities, or relationships before you find the right combination of people who truly understand and encourage your journey. The investment in building genuine support pays off dramatically when you face challenges, celebrate victories, or need encouragement to maintain your progress over the long term.

Chapter 4 Make Your Move

These exercises help you assess your current relationships, identify potential sources of support and sabotage, practice boundary-setting skills, and build a network of people who genuinely support your transformation and long-term success.

Complete a relationship assessment by creating three lists of people in your life: supporters who consistently encourage your health goals and respect your choices, neutral parties who don't strongly impact your journey either positively or negatively, and potential saboteurs who have shown resistance to your surgery decision or patterns of undermining behavior. Include family members, friends, coworkers, neighbors, and anyone else who has regular contact with you during this transformation.

Identify specific sabotaging behaviors you've experienced or expect to encounter by writing down examples of food sabotage, emotional undermining, social exclusion, identity denial, or relationship manipulation from people in your life. Include direct quotes when possible and note how each behavior made you feel and how it affected your confidence or progress toward your goals.

Create your boundary script by writing specific

responses to common boundary violations you anticipate facing. Include responses for people who comment on your food choices, ask intrusive questions about your surgery, offer foods you can't eat, make jokes about your appearance, or create guilt about your lifestyle changes. Practice these responses until you can deliver them confidently and calmly.

Design your support system map by identifying what types of help you need during different phases of your journey and which people in your life might be able to provide each type of support. Include practical help like meal preparation and transportation, emotional support like encouragement and listening, informational support like advice and resources, and social support like activity partners and celebration companions.

Practice boundary-setting conversations by role-playing difficult scenarios with a trusted friend or family member who supports your goals. Practice setting limits on food-related comments, declining invitations that don't support your success, asking for what you need from important relationships, and responding to criticism or sabotage with confidence and clarity.

Develop your support network expansion plan by

identifying places, activities, and communities where you might meet people who share your values around health, personal growth, and positive lifestyle changes. This might include fitness classes, support groups, volunteer organizations, hobby clubs, or professional development activities that align with your interests and goals.

Create your relationship maintenance strategy by planning how you'll nurture supportive relationships, address problems with neutral parties who could become more supportive, and limit contact with people who consistently undermine your progress. Include specific actions like regular check-ins with supporters, clear communication about your needs, and consequences for continued sabotaging behavior.

Finally, establish your support system check-in routine by scheduling monthly reviews of your relationships to assess which connections are supporting your success and which ones need attention or adjustment. Include questions about who makes you feel encouraged versus discouraged, which relationships energize versus drain you, and what changes you need to make to protect your progress and maintain your motivation.

Use these tools consistently throughout your transformation journey, adjusting your approach as relationships evolve and your needs change. The relationship skills you develop now will serve you not only during your weight loss phase but throughout your entire life as you continue to grow and change in positive ways.

Chapter 5: Busting Myths

The myths about weight loss surgery are everywhere, and they're probably living in your head right now, whispering lies that make you question your decision and doubt your ability to succeed. These myths get passed around like gospel truth in family conversations, workplace discussions, and internet forums, but most of them are based on outdated information, fear-based thinking, or complete misunderstandings about how modern surgery actually works.

You've probably heard that surgery is the easy way out, that most people gain all their weight back, that you'll never be able to eat normally again, that complications are common and dangerous, or that you should be able to lose weight naturally if you just had more willpower and discipline. These myths feel true because they get repeated so often and because they tap into the shame and guilt that most people carry about their weight and their previous attempts at losing it. But believing these lies keeps you stuck in patterns that don't work, prevents you from using tools that could change your life, and makes you feel like a failure before you even start your transformation journey.

The truth about weight loss surgery is much more encouraging than the myths suggest, but it's also more complex than the fairy tale success stories that make it sound effortless. Understanding the real facts helps you make informed decisions, set realistic expectations, and approach your surgery with confidence instead of fear or shame about needing help to achieve your health goals.

The 'Easy Way Out' Lie

The biggest myth about weight loss surgery is that it's an easy solution that requires no effort, discipline, or lifestyle changes, and this lie does tremendous damage to people who are considering surgery because it makes them feel guilty for wanting to use an effective tool instead of continuing to struggle with methods that haven't worked for them. The truth is that surgery is one of the hardest things you'll ever do, not because the procedure itself is difficult, but because it requires you to change every single habit, coping mechanism, and relationship with food that you've developed over your entire lifetime.

Surgery doesn't eliminate hunger, cravings, or the emotional triggers that led to overeating in the first place. It creates a smaller stomach that gets full faster and stays full longer, but you still have to choose what foods to put in that smaller space, still have to deal with stress and emotions without using food as comfort, still have to develop new social patterns that don't revolve around eating, and still have to maintain these changes for the rest of your life to keep the weight off.

The physical restriction from surgery helps tremendously with portion control, but it doesn't automatically make you choose protein over cookies, vegetables over chips, or water over soda. You still have to learn about nutrition, plan your meals, prepare healthy foods, and make conscious decisions about what to eat at every single meal and snack for years after your surgery.

Surgery doesn't fix emotional eating patterns or teach you new ways to cope with stress, boredom, sadness, anger, or celebration. You still have to develop alternative coping strategies, learn to sit with uncomfortable emotions without feeding them, build new social connections that don't center around food, and create celebration rituals that don't involve eating.

The lifestyle changes required for surgical success are more demanding than most diet programs because they're permanent rather than temporary. You can't take a break from your eating plan when you get tired of it, can't have cheat days when you want to indulge, can't go back to old eating patterns when life gets stressful, and can't ignore your nutritional needs without risking serious health consequences.

Surgery patients have to take vitamins for life, get regular blood work to monitor their nutritional status, follow specific eating guidelines about portion sizes and food combinations, avoid certain foods that can cause complications, and maintain regular follow-up appointments with their surgical team to ensure their continued health and success.

The social and emotional challenges of transformation require just as much work as the physical changes. You have to learn to handle other people's reactions to your weight loss, navigate social situations where you can't eat the way you used to, deal with relationship changes as your confidence grows, and maintain your motivation when the initial excitement of rapid weight loss fades and the real work of maintenance begins.

People who succeed long-term with weight loss surgery work harder at maintaining their health than most people work at anything in their lives. They plan every meal, track their protein intake, schedule regular exercise, attend support group meetings, manage their stress without using food, and make their health a priority even when it's inconvenient or socially awkward.

The idea that surgery is easy comes from people who see the dramatic weight loss results without understanding the daily discipline, planning, and commitment required to achieve and maintain those results. They see someone eating small portions and assume the surgery automatically controls their eating, but they don't see the mental work of choosing those portions, planning those meals, and resisting the urge to eat more when emotions or social pressure suggest otherwise.

Surgery is a tool, not a solution, and like any tool, its effectiveness depends on how skillfully and consistently you use it. A hammer doesn't build a house by itself, and surgery doesn't create lasting weight loss without your active participation in changing the habits and patterns that contributed to weight gain in the first place.

The people who call surgery the easy way out usually haven't struggled with significant weight issues themselves, haven't tried and failed at multiple diet attempts, haven't dealt with the medical complications of obesity, and haven't faced the daily challenges of living in a body that limits their activities and affects their quality of life. Their judgment comes from ignorance rather than experience, and their opinions shouldn't carry more weight than the advice of medical professionals who understand the complexity of obesity and the effectiveness of surgical treatment.

Choosing surgery means choosing the hard work of permanent lifestyle change over the temporary fixes that haven't worked in the past. It means admitting that you need help and being willing to use every available tool to succeed rather than continuing to struggle with willpower alone. It means taking responsibility for your health in the most comprehensive way possible, not taking the easy way out.

Failure Fears and Success Stories

The fear of failing at weight loss surgery haunts most people considering the procedure because they've experienced so many diet failures in the past, but the statistics about surgical success are dramatically different from the statistics about traditional weight loss methods, and understanding these numbers helps put your fears into perspective while building confidence in your ability to succeed.

Traditional diet programs have a long-term success rate of less than five percent, meaning that fewer than one in twenty people who lose significant weight through dieting alone maintain that loss for five years or more. Weight loss surgery, by contrast, has long-term success rates of sixty to eighty percent depending on the procedure, with most people maintaining significant weight loss and health improvements for decades after their surgery.

The definition of success with surgery is also more realistic than the all-or-nothing thinking that characterizes diet culture. Surgical success is typically defined as losing fifty percent or more of excess body weight and maintaining that loss, along with improvements in obesity-related health conditions like diabetes, high blood pressure, and sleep apnea.

This means that someone who weighs three hundred pounds before surgery and loses one hundred pounds is considered successful even if they don't reach their ideal body weight, because they've achieved significant health improvements and dramatically reduced their risk of obesity-related complications. Diet culture, by contrast, often treats anything less than reaching goal weight as failure, even when substantial health benefits have been achieved.

The people who regain weight after surgery usually do so because they return to old eating patterns rather than because the surgery stops working, and even when some regain occurs, most people maintain significant weight loss compared to their pre-surgery weight. Complete weight regain to pre-surgery levels is rare and usually indicates serious underlying issues like untreated eating disorders, substance abuse problems, or failure to follow post-surgery guidelines.

Your past diet failures don't predict your surgical outcomes because surgery changes the physical and hormonal factors that make long-term weight maintenance so difficult with traditional methods. Surgery reduces the stomach hormone ghrelin that triggers hunger, increases hormones like GLP-1 that promote satiety, and creates physical restriction that makes overeating uncomfortable rather than relying on willpower alone to control portions.

The rapid initial weight loss that occurs in the first six to twelve months after surgery creates momentum and motivation that helps establish new habits during the period when they're most likely to stick. This is completely different from the slow, frustrating process of traditional dieting where people often give up before seeing significant results because the changes feel too small and too slow to maintain motivation.

Surgery also provides ongoing accountability through

regular follow-up appointments, blood work monitoring, and the physical consequences of eating inappropriate foods, creating external structure that supports long-term success rather than relying entirely on internal motivation and discipline that can fluctuate with mood, stress levels, and life circumstances.

The people who succeed with surgery long-term share certain characteristics that you can develop regardless of your past diet history: they attend follow-up appointments regularly, take their vitamins consistently, prioritize protein at every meal, stay connected with support systems, address emotional eating patterns, maintain regular physical activity, and treat their surgery as the beginning of a lifelong commitment to health rather than a quick fix.

Success with surgery looks different for different people and doesn't always match the dramatic before-and-after photos you see on social media. Some people lose weight quickly and reach their goal weight within two years, others lose more slowly but achieve significant health improvements, and still others experience periods of weight loss, maintenance, and minor regain while still maintaining overall success compared to their pre-surgery health and weight.

The fear of failure often becomes a self-fulfilling

prophecy when it prevents people from fully committing to the lifestyle changes that surgery requires. People who approach surgery expecting to fail are less likely to follow through on nutritional guidelines, attend support groups, or address emotional eating patterns because they've already decided that success isn't possible for them.

Building confidence in your ability to succeed requires focusing on the factors you can control rather than worrying about statistical outcomes you can't influence. You can control your choice of surgeon, your commitment to following post-surgery guidelines, your willingness to address emotional eating patterns, your participation in support systems, and your approach to setbacks and challenges that inevitably occur during any major lifestyle change.

Remember that surgical success is measured over years and decades rather than months, and that maintaining significant weight loss and health improvements over time is more important than achieving perfect results quickly. The people who succeed long-term focus on progress rather than perfection, celebrate small victories along the way, and treat setbacks as learning opportunities rather than evidence of failure.

Your past diet attempts taught you valuable lessons

about what doesn't work for long-term weight management, and that knowledge actually increases your chances of surgical success because you understand the limitations of willpower-based approaches and the importance of having tools that provide ongoing support for maintaining healthy habits over time.

Body Image Reality Check

The fantasy about how your body will look after weight loss surgery often sets people up for disappointment because the reality of dramatic weight loss includes changes that nobody talks about during the excitement of planning your transformation. Understanding what to realistically expect helps you prepare mentally for the actual experience of living in a rapidly changing body rather than being shocked by outcomes that are completely normal but rarely discussed.

Loose skin is the most common concern people have about rapid weight loss, and the reality is that some loose skin is likely if you lose a significant amount of weight quickly, especially if you're older, have been overweight for many years, or lose more than one hundred pounds. The amount of loose skin varies dramatically from person to person based on genetics, age, skin elasticity, how much weight you lose, and how quickly you lose it.

Some loose skin will tighten up over time as your body adjusts to its new size, especially if you're younger and haven't been overweight for decades, but significant loose skin often requires surgical removal if you want a smooth, tight appearance. This doesn't mean you'll look terrible or that you should avoid weight loss surgery because of loose skin concerns, but it does mean adjusting your expectations about what your body will look like at your goal weight.

Most people find that loose skin is a minor inconvenience compared to the health benefits, increased energy, improved mobility, and enhanced quality of life that come with significant weight loss. Loose skin can be hidden under clothing, managed with supportive undergarments, or removed surgically if it bothers you enough to justify additional procedures, but it doesn't negate the tremendous benefits of achieving a healthier weight.

Your body shape will change in ways you might not expect as you lose weight because fat comes off in patterns determined by genetics rather than your preferences. You might lose weight in your face and arms before your stomach and thighs, or find that your proportions look different than you imagined when you were planning your transformation. Some people discover that they have broader shoulders or narrower hips than they realized when those features were hidden by excess weight.

The speed of weight loss after surgery can make it difficult for your brain to keep up with your changing body, leading to a disconnect between how you look and how you feel about your appearance. You might still see your old body when you look in the mirror, avoid trying on smaller clothes even when your current ones are too big, or feel surprised when people comment on your weight loss because you don't feel like you look that different.

This body image lag is completely normal and usually resolves over time as your brain adjusts to your new appearance, but it can be frustrating when you expected to feel immediately confident and comfortable in your smaller body. Some people benefit from taking progress photos regularly, trying on old clothes to see the difference, or working with counselors who specialize in body image issues during major weight loss.

Your relationship with clothes and shopping will change dramatically as you lose weight, and this process can be both exciting and overwhelming. You'll need new clothes multiple times during your weight loss phase, which can be expensive and time-consuming, and you might struggle with choosing styles that flatter your changing body or feel confident wearing clothes that show your figure instead of hiding it.

Many people go through a phase of not knowing how to dress their new body because they've spent years choosing clothes based on camouflaging their size rather than expressing their personal style. Learning to shop for fit rather than size, experimenting with styles you couldn't wear at higher weights, and developing confidence in showing your figure takes time and practice.

The attention you receive about your weight loss can feel uncomfortable even when it's positive, especially if you're not used to people commenting on your appearance or if the attention makes you feel like people only value you for how you look rather than who you are as a person. Some people struggle with resentment about getting more positive attention at lower weights, wondering why people treat them better now than they did before surgery.

Your energy levels and physical capabilities will improve dramatically as you lose weight, but the adjustment to having a body that can do things you couldn't do before takes time and mental preparation. You might feel nervous about trying new activities, unsure about your physical limits, or overwhelmed by having more energy than you've had in years.

Building a positive relationship with your post-surgery body requires focusing on function rather than just appearance, celebrating what your body can do rather than obsessing over how it looks, and practicing self-compassion during the adjustment period when everything feels different and sometimes uncomfortable. Your body has been through a major transformation, and it deserves appreciation for its resilience and adaptability rather than criticism for not looking exactly like the fantasy version you imagined.

Remember that your worth isn't determined by how your body looks at any weight, and that the goal of surgery is health and improved quality of life rather than achieving a perfect appearance. The confidence that comes from feeling strong, energetic, and capable in your body matters more than having a body that looks like a magazine cover, and learning to appreciate your transformed body for all it can do helps you maintain a positive relationship with yourself throughout the ongoing changes.

The Identity Shift Truth

Losing a significant amount of weight doesn't just

change how you look, it fundamentally alters how you see yourself and how other people see you, creating an identity shift that can feel both liberating and terrifying as you navigate becoming a different version of yourself while trying to stay connected to your authentic core. This transformation goes much deeper than clothing sizes and compliments, touching every aspect of how you move through the world and relate to other people.

Your sense of self has probably been intertwined with your weight for years or decades, and when that weight disappears rapidly, you might feel lost about who you are without it. If you've thought of yourself as the funny fat friend, the reliable caretaker who focuses on others instead of herself, or the person who stays in the background and avoids attention, those identities might not fit anymore when you're getting compliments and feeling more confident in your body.

The roles you've played in your family, friend groups, and work environment might shift as your confidence grows and your priorities change. You might find yourself speaking up more in meetings, setting boundaries you never enforced before, pursuing opportunities you avoided when you felt self-conscious about your appearance, or expecting better treatment from people who got used to you accepting less than you deserved.

These changes can feel exciting and empowering, but they can also create anxiety about whether you're still the same person people fell in love with, whether your relationships will survive your transformation, and whether you'll lose important parts of your personality along with the weight. The fear of becoming someone you don't recognize or someone others don't like can make you unconsciously sabotage your progress or downplay your achievements to avoid dealing with identity changes.

Your relationship with food has probably been central to your identity in ways you might not fully realize until surgery forces you to change those patterns. If you've been the person who brings the best dishes to potlucks, knows all the good restaurants in town, or bonds with people over shared meals and cooking experiences, losing that connection can feel like losing an important part of who you are.

The social aspects of your identity might shift as you become more comfortable in group settings, more willing to try new activities, or more interested in pursuing hobbies and interests you avoided when you felt limited by your weight. This expansion of your social world can be wonderful, but it can also create guilt about outgrowing old friendships or anxiety about fitting in with new groups of people.

Your professional identity might change as you gain confidence to pursue promotions, speak up in meetings, network with colleagues, or take on leadership roles you avoided when you felt self-conscious about your appearance. Some people find that their career prospects improve dramatically after weight loss, not necessarily because of appearance discrimination, but because their increased confidence and energy make them more effective and visible in their work environments.

The way you handle conflict, stress, and difficult emotions will necessarily change when food is no longer your primary coping mechanism, and developing new ways to manage these challenges becomes part of your evolving identity. You might discover that you're more assertive, more willing to address problems directly, or more capable of handling stress than you realized when you were using food to numb difficult feelings.

Your romantic and sexual identity might shift dramatically as you become more comfortable with physical intimacy, more confident about your attractiveness, or more willing to pursue relationships you avoided when you felt unworthy of love and attention.

These changes can enhance existing relationships or create tension if your partner isn't prepared for your increased confidence and changed priorities.

The key to navigating identity changes successfully is remembering that your core values, personality traits, and fundamental character don't change with your weight. You're still the same person who loves your children, cares about your friends, has the same sense of humor, enjoys the same hobbies, and holds the same beliefs about what matters in life. Weight loss reveals and enhances who you already are rather than creating a completely different person.

Allow yourself to grow and change without feeling guilty about outgrowing old patterns or relationships that no longer serve your health and happiness. Growth is a natural part of life, and the changes that come with weight loss surgery are generally positive developments that help you become more authentic and confident rather than fundamentally different.

Practice staying connected to your values and priorities throughout your transformation so that your identity changes feel like natural evolution rather than losing yourself. The person you become at your goal weight should feel like the best version of who you've always been rather than a stranger you don't recognize or relate to.

Communicate with important people in your life about the changes you're experiencing and reassure them that your love and commitment to them remain constant even as other aspects of your life shift. Help them understand that your increased confidence and changed priorities make you a better partner, parent, friend, and colleague rather than a different person who no longer cares about the relationships that matter most.

Remember that identity shifts take time to integrate and that feeling unsure about who you are during periods of rapid change is completely normal and temporary. Most people find that their sense of self stabilizes as their weight stabilizes and they adjust to living in their transformed body with their enhanced capabilities and confidence.

Chapter 5 Make Your Move

These exercises help you identify and challenge the myths that might be limiting your confidence, set realistic expectations for your transformation, prepare for identity changes, and build a foundation of facts and self-awareness that supports your long-term success with weight loss surgery.

Create your myth-busting fact sheet by researching and writing down accurate statistics about weight loss surgery success rates, complication rates, long-term outcomes, and lifestyle requirements. Include information from reputable medical sources about your specific procedure, and compare these facts to the myths you've heard from friends, family members, or online sources. Keep this fact sheet handy for times when doubt or criticism makes you question your decision.

Complete a past diet analysis by listing every significant weight loss attempt you've made in the past, including what method you used, how much weight you lost, how long you maintained the loss, and what factors contributed to regaining weight. Look for patterns in what didn't work long-term and identify how surgery addresses those specific challenges differently than traditional diet approaches.

Write your realistic expectations document by describing what you hope surgery will change in your life and what you understand will remain the same or require ongoing effort. Include expectations about weight loss timeline, body changes, loose skin possibilities, lifestyle adjustments, relationship impacts, and the ongoing work required for long-term success. Review this regularly to stay grounded in reality rather than fantasy outcomes.

Develop your body image preparation plan by taking current photos from multiple angles, writing about your current relationship with your body, and setting intentions for how you want to think and feel about your body as it changes. Include strategies for handling loose skin, adjusting to compliments and attention, shopping for new clothes, and maintaining a positive relationship with your appearance throughout your transformation.

Complete an identity exploration exercise by writing about who you are beyond your weight, what roles you play in your relationships and work life, what values guide your decisions, and what aspects of your personality you want to maintain regardless of how your body changes. Include fears about losing important parts of yourself and excitement about aspects of your identity that might expand or strengthen as you gain confidence.

Create your success definition worksheet by writing your personal definition of success with weight loss surgery, including specific weight loss goals, health improvements you hope to achieve, lifestyle changes you want to make, and quality of life enhancements that matter most to you. Make sure your definition is realistic and based on your individual circumstances rather than comparing yourself to other people's results.

Build your confidence evidence file by documenting your strengths, past successes in overcoming challenges, support systems you have in place, and preparation steps you've taken for surgery. Include evidence that contradicts fears about failure and supports your ability to succeed with the lifestyle changes that surgery requires. Add to this file regularly as you demonstrate your commitment to your health goals.

Finally, establish your reality check routine by scheduling monthly reviews of your progress, expectations, and mindset throughout your weight loss journey. Include questions about whether your expectations are realistic, how your identity is evolving, what myths or fears are affecting your confidence, and what adjustments you need to make to stay grounded in facts rather than fears or fantasies about your transformation.

Use these tools consistently to maintain a realistic, positive, and fact-based approach to your weight loss surgery journey. The mental preparation you do now creates a foundation of confidence and realistic expectations that supports your success throughout your transformation and helps you navigate challenges with wisdom rather than being derailed by myths or unrealistic expectations.

Chapter 6: The Surgery Countdown

The final weeks before your surgery date feel like the longest and shortest time of your life all at once, and your brain starts playing tricks on you in ways that can either prepare you for success or send you into a panic spiral that makes everything harder than it needs to be. Your surgery date sits there on the calendar like a mountain you're about to climb, and every day that passes brings a mix of excitement about finally taking action and terror about everything that could go wrong or change in ways you can't predict.

This countdown period tests every bit of mental preparation you've done up to this point. Your emotions swing from confidence to fear to excitement to doubt, sometimes all in the same hour, and people around you start treating you differently because they know something big is about to happen in your life. Some days you feel ready to conquer the world and other days you wonder if you're making the biggest mistake of your life, and both feelings can be true at the same time because you're facing something that will change everything about how you live, eat, and move through the world.

The pre-surgery diet phase kicks in and suddenly you're getting a preview of how different your relationship with food is about to become, which can feel overwhelming when you're already dealing with appointment schedules, work arrangements, childcare plans, and a thousand other details that need to be handled before you can focus entirely on healing and recovery. Your brain wants to control every possible variable, but the reality is that some things are beyond your control and the best thing you can do is prepare what you can and trust the process for everything else.

The people who handle this countdown period well focus their energy on the practical preparations that actually make a difference while developing mental strategies that keep them calm and confident instead of anxious and overwhelmed. They use this time to build habits that will serve them after surgery, practice coping skills they'll need during recovery, and create an environment that supports their success rather than trying to predict and prevent every possible challenge they might face.

Final Weeks Mental Preparation

Your mind becomes your biggest ally or your worst

enemy during the final weeks before surgery, and learning to manage the intense emotions that surface during this time determines whether you approach your surgery date with confidence and peace or with panic and regret about your decision. The mental chatter gets louder as your surgery date approaches because your brain interprets the upcoming change as a potential threat and starts generating every possible reason why this might not work out the way you hope.

The "what if" thoughts multiply like rabbits during this phase, and they range from reasonable concerns about recovery and complications to completely irrational fears about never being able to enjoy food again or becoming a different person that nobody recognizes or likes.

Your brain might start replaying every diet failure from your past and suggesting that surgery will just be another temporary fix that doesn't last, or it might focus on horror stories you've heard about complications and convince you that you're going to be the statistical outlier who has serious problems. These thoughts feel urgent and important, but most of them are just your nervous system's way of trying to protect you from change, even when that change is exactly what you need to improve your health and quality of life.

The key to managing pre-surgery mental chaos is distinguishing between productive preparation thoughts and unproductive worry spirals that drain your energy without helping you get ready for success. Productive thoughts lead to helpful actions like organizing your recovery space, stocking up on approved foods, arranging help from family and friends, and reviewing your post-surgery eating guidelines so you feel prepared and confident about what comes next.

Unproductive worry spirals involve repeatedly imagining worst-case scenarios, reading negative stories online, trying to control outcomes that are beyond your influence, or second-guessing your decision based on other people's fears rather than your own carefully considered choice. When you catch yourself in a worry spiral, redirect your attention to concrete actions you can take to prepare for success rather than trying to predict and prevent every possible problem.

Create a daily mental preparation routine that includes activities proven to reduce anxiety and build confidence, such as deep breathing exercises, positive visualization, journaling about your goals and motivations, or meditation practices that help you stay centered in the present moment rather than getting lost in fearful predictions about the future. Consistency matters more than duration, so even five minutes of daily mental preparation can make a significant difference in your emotional state as surgery approaches.

Practice positive self-talk by consciously replacing fearful thoughts with more balanced, realistic perspectives that acknowledge both the challenges and benefits of your upcoming transformation. Instead of "What if something goes wrong," try "I've chosen an experienced surgeon and I'm prepared to handle whatever comes up." Instead of "I always fail at weight loss," try "Surgery gives me tools I've never had before, and I'm committed to using them effectively."

Limit your exposure to negative information and unsupportive people during this vulnerable time when your emotional defenses are lower than usual and you're more susceptible to other people's fears and doubts. Stop reading online forums that focus on complications and problems, avoid people who want to debate your decision or share horror stories, and create boundaries around discussions of your surgery with anyone who isn't genuinely supportive of your choice.

Connect with your support system regularly during these final weeks, reaching out to people who encourage your decision and remind you of your strength and capability when doubt creeps in. This might include friends and family members who celebrate your courage, online communities of people who have had successful surgery experiences, or healthcare providers who can answer questions and provide reassurance about normal pre-surgery anxiety.

Focus on your "why" whenever fear threatens to overwhelm your confidence, reminding yourself of all the reasons you decided surgery was the right choice for your health, happiness, and quality of life. Review the goals you wrote down when you first started considering surgery, look at photos that remind you of activities you want to be able to do, and reconnect with the vision of the life you're working toward rather than getting stuck in fear about the process of getting there.

Remember that feeling nervous about surgery doesn't mean you're not ready for it or that you've made the wrong decision. Anxiety is a normal response to any major life change, and the fact that you're taking this step seriously enough to feel nervous actually demonstrates your maturity and realistic understanding of what you're about to undertake. The goal isn't to eliminate all nervousness, but to keep anxiety at a manageable level that doesn't interfere with your preparation or your confidence in your decision.

Use this countdown period to strengthen your mental resilience and coping skills because the emotional tools you develop now will serve you throughout your entire transformation journey. The ability to manage anxiety, challenge negative thoughts, stay connected to your goals, and maintain confidence in the face of uncertainty becomes crucial not just for surgery preparation, but for navigating all the changes and challenges that come with losing weight and rebuilding your relationship with food and your body.

Practical Prep That Reduces Anxiety

Taking control of the practical details you can manage helps calm your mind by giving you concrete actions to focus on instead of abstract worries about things beyond your control, and the more prepared your environment is for your return from surgery, the more you can focus your mental energy on healing rather than scrambling to handle basic needs while you're recovering from a major procedure.

Your recovery space becomes your headquarters for the first few weeks after surgery, so set it up like a comfortable command center where everything you need is within easy reach and the environment promotes rest and healing rather than stress and frustration.

Arrange your bedroom or main recovery area so that you can access water, medications, protein drinks, approved snacks, entertainment options, phone chargers, and comfort items without having to climb stairs, bend over, or lift heavy objects that might strain your incisions or cause discomfort during the early healing phase.

Stock your kitchen with foods that meet your post-surgery requirements and that you actually enjoy eating, because the last thing you want is to come home from surgery and realize you have nothing appealing that fits your new eating plan. This includes protein shakes or powders that taste good to you, clear broths that provide flavor and comfort, sugar-free beverages that keep you hydrated, soft foods for the pureed phase, and eventually solid foods that are high in protein and low in sugar and refined carbohydrates.

Prepare several days' worth of meals in advance and freeze them in single-serving portions so you don't have to cook or make food decisions when you're tired and healing. Focus on simple, protein-rich options like egg salad, tuna salad, cottage cheese with fruit, Greek yogurt, soft-cooked chicken, and pureed soups that meet your nutritional needs without requiring much preparation or cleanup.

Organize your medications, vitamins, and supplements in a way that makes it easy to take them consistently even when you're feeling tired or uncomfortable. Use a pill organizer to sort your daily medications, set phone alarms to remind you when to take different supplements, and create a simple tracking system to make sure you're meeting all your nutritional requirements during the critical healing period.

Arrange for practical help with household tasks, childcare, pet care, grocery shopping, and transportation during your recovery period so you can focus entirely on following your post-surgery guidelines rather than trying to maintain your normal responsibilities while your body is healing. Be specific about what help you need and when you need it, and don't be afraid to ask for more support than you think you might need because it's better to have help available and not need it than to need help and not have it arranged.

Prepare your work situation by arranging time off, delegating important responsibilities, and setting up systems that allow your workplace to function smoothly without you during your recovery period. Clear communication about your expected return date and any limitations you might have when you come back helps prevent work stress from interfering with your healing process.

Create a communication plan for keeping important people updated on your progress without having to repeat the same information multiple times or deal with constant phone calls and text messages when you need to rest. This might include designating one family member to send updates to everyone else, creating a group text for close family and friends, or using social media to share general updates without having individual conversations with everyone who wants to know how you're doing.

Pack your hospital bag with items that make you feel comfortable and prepared, including loose-fitting clothes for the trip home, comfortable slippers, personal hygiene items, phone chargers, entertainment options for potential waiting periods, and any comfort items that help you feel more at ease in medical settings. Check with your surgical team about what items are recommended or restricted so you don't bring anything that interferes with your care.

Prepare your transportation arrangements for surgery day and follow-up appointments, making sure you have reliable rides arranged and backup plans in case your primary transportation falls through. You won't be able to drive for a period after surgery, and having transportation stress during your recovery period can interfere with your healing and compliance with follow-up care requirements.

Set up your insurance and financial arrangements in advance so you don't have to deal with paperwork and billing issues while you're recovering. Understand what costs are covered, what you'll be responsible for paying, and how to handle any billing questions that arise after your surgery so these practical concerns don't create additional stress during your healing period.

Create backup plans for potential complications or delays in your recovery timeline, including arrangements for extended help if you need it, flexibility in your work return date, and contingency plans for childcare or other responsibilities if your healing takes longer than expected. Having these backup plans in place reduces anxiety about what-if scenarios and helps you feel prepared for various possible outcomes.

The time you spend on practical preparation pays dividends in reduced stress and smoother recovery because you've eliminated as many potential problems and inconveniences as possible before they can interfere with your healing process. When your environment is set up to support your success and your practical needs are handled by other people or advance planning, you can dedicate your energy to following your post-surgery guidelines and developing the new habits that will support your long-term transformation.

Managing the Food Farewell Tour

The urge to eat all your favorite foods one last time before surgery is almost universal among pre-surgery patients, and this "farewell tour" mentality can sabotage your pre-surgery diet requirements, set you up for post-surgery regret and cravings, and reinforce the exact mindset about food that contributed to your weight struggles in the first place. Understanding why this urge happens and developing strategies to manage it helps you approach surgery with a healthier relationship with food rather than a sense of deprivation and loss.

The farewell tour impulse comes from scarcity thinking that treats your pre-surgery diet restrictions as the beginning of a lifetime of deprivation rather than the start of a healthier relationship with food that includes enjoyment, satisfaction, and freedom from the compulsive eating patterns that kept you stuck at an unhealthy weight.

Your brain interprets the upcoming changes as a threat to your access to comfort and pleasure, triggering urges to stockpile experiences with foods you think you'll never be able to enjoy again, but this thinking is based on the false belief that your worth and happiness depend on your ability to eat large quantities of certain foods rather than on the satisfaction that comes from eating appropriate amounts of foods that nourish your body and support your goals.

The reality is that you'll be able to eat most foods after surgery, just in smaller quantities and with more attention to how they affect your body and your weight management goals. The restriction isn't about never eating certain foods again, it's about eating them in portions and frequencies that support your health rather than undermine it, and developing the skills to enjoy food without using it as your primary source of comfort, entertainment, or emotional regulation.

Engaging in a farewell tour often makes the transition to post-surgery eating more difficult because it reinforces cravings for foods that don't support your goals, creates guilt and regret about overeating right before making a commitment to healthier habits, and can interfere with the pre-surgery diet requirements that prepare your body for the procedure and reduce surgical risks.

Instead of focusing on what you're giving up, shift your attention to what you're gaining through surgery and the lifestyle changes it makes possible. You're gaining the ability to feel satisfied with appropriate portions, freedom from constant thoughts about food and weight, energy for activities you've been avoiding, confidence in your body and appearance, and the health improvements that come with maintaining a weight that supports your wellbeing rather than threatening it.

Practice mindful eating during your pre-surgery diet phase by paying attention to hunger and fullness cues, eating slowly and without distractions, and focusing on the flavors and textures of foods rather than eating quickly or mindlessly. These skills become crucial after surgery when your stomach is smaller and eating too quickly or without attention can cause discomfort, so developing them now makes your post-surgery transition smoother.

Explore new foods and recipes that fit your post-surgery eating plan so you're building excitement about the foods you can eat rather than mourning the foods you'll eat less frequently. Experiment with protein-rich recipes, try new vegetables and preparation methods, and discover healthy versions of foods you enjoy so your post-surgery eating feels like an adventure rather than a restriction.

Address the emotional aspects of your relationship with food by developing alternative sources of comfort, celebration, and stress relief that don't involve eating.

Practice using these alternatives during your pre-surgery phase so they feel familiar and effective when you need them most during your recovery and adjustment period after surgery.

If you do choose to have farewell meals with certain foods, do so mindfully and in moderation rather than engaging in binge eating that makes you feel physically and emotionally worse. Pay attention to how these foods actually make you feel, both physically and emotionally, and use that information to reinforce your commitment to healthier choices rather than romanticizing foods that don't actually support your wellbeing.

Focus on saying goodbye to eating behaviors rather than specific foods, recognizing that what you're really changing is your relationship with food rather than eliminating entire categories of foods from your life forever. You're saying goodbye to eating when you're not hungry, eating past the point of satisfaction, using food to manage emotions, and eating in ways that damage your health rather than support it.

Create new food traditions and rituals that align with your post-surgery lifestyle, such as trying one new healthy recipe each week, having a weekly meal prep session, or celebrating special occasions with experiences rather than food-centered activities. Building excitement about these new traditions helps you feel like you're moving toward something positive rather than just giving up things you enjoy.

Remember that the goal of surgery isn't to eliminate all food enjoyment from your life, but to help you develop a balanced relationship with food where eating serves your health and happiness rather than controlling your thoughts, emotions, and behaviors. The restriction that surgery provides helps you break free from compulsive eating patterns so you can actually enjoy food more because you're eating it by choice rather than compulsion, and in amounts that make you feel good rather than uncomfortable or guilty.

Use your pre-surgery diet period as practice for the mindful, intentional eating habits that will support your long-term success rather than as a last chance to indulge in behaviors that haven't served your health goals. The mental shift from scarcity to abundance thinking about food happens gradually, but it starts with recognizing that true food freedom comes from eating in ways that support your goals rather than undermine them.

Surgery Day Confidence Boosters

The actual day of surgery brings a unique combination of excitement, nervousness, and surreal disbelief that this day you've been planning for months has finally arrived, and having specific strategies to stay calm and confident helps you approach the procedure with peace rather than panic, trust rather than terror, and focus on your goals rather than your fears about everything that could go wrong.

Start your surgery day with a morning routine that makes you feel grounded and connected to your reasons for choosing this path rather than rushing around in a panic or lying in bed catastrophizing about potential complications.

This might include meditation or prayer, reading your written goals and motivations, looking at photos that remind you of activities you want to be able to do, or simply taking a few minutes to breathe deeply and remind yourself that you've prepared thoroughly for this day and you're ready to take this important step toward better health and quality of life.

Bring comfort items to the hospital that help you feel more like yourself and less like just another patient going through a medical procedure. This might include a favorite pillow or blanket, photos of people you love, music that calms or inspires you, or any small personal items that provide comfort and remind you of your identity beyond your weight and your surgery.

Focus on the immediate next step rather than trying to think through your entire recovery timeline or imagine how you'll feel weeks or months from now. Your only job on surgery day is to show up, follow the medical team's instructions, and trust the process that you've carefully planned and prepared for over the past months.

Practice the breathing and relaxation techniques you've been developing during your pre-surgery preparation period, using them to stay calm during waiting periods, medical preparations, and any moments when anxiety starts to build. These techniques work best when they're familiar and practiced rather than something you're trying for the first time when you're already feeling stressed.

Remind yourself of your surgical team's qualifications and experience, the research you did in choosing your surgeon, and the preparation you've done to ensure the best possible outcome. You didn't choose this surgery casually or impulsively, and you didn't choose your medical team randomly, so trust the careful decision-making process that brought you to this day.

Visualize your recovery and transformation process going smoothly, imagining yourself following your post-surgery guidelines successfully, healing well, and achieving the health and quality of life improvements that motivated you to have surgery. Positive visualization helps calm your nervous system and reinforces your confidence in your ability to succeed with the lifestyle changes that surgery requires.

Connect with your support system before surgery, whether through phone calls, text messages, or simply knowing that people who love you are thinking of you and rooting for your success. You don't have to handle this day entirely on your own, and drawing strength from people who believe in you can boost your confidence when your own feels shaky.

Avoid last-minute research about complications, success rates, or other people's surgery experiences because this information is more likely to increase anxiety than provide helpful preparation at this point. You've already done your research and made your decision, and surgery day is about trusting that process rather than second-guessing it.

Remember that thousands of people have successful weight loss surgery every year, that complications are rare and usually manageable when they do occur, and that your surgical team is trained to handle any situation that might arise during your procedure. You're not the first person to have this surgery, and you won't be the last, and the routine nature of these procedures for your medical team should provide reassurance about their expertise and preparedness.

Focus on the positive changes you're working toward rather than the risks you're trying to avoid, keeping your attention on your goals for improved health, increased energy, enhanced mobility, and better quality of life rather than getting stuck in fear-based thinking about everything that could go wrong. The energy you put toward positive outcomes is more helpful than energy spent worrying about negative possibilities.

Trust your body's ability to heal and adapt to the changes that surgery creates, recognizing that your body has been healing from injuries and adapting to changes your entire life and that this surgery is another challenge that your body is equipped to handle with proper medical support and your commitment to following recovery guidelines.

Keep your perspective on the bigger picture of your transformation journey, remembering that surgery day is just one day in a process that will unfold over months and years, and that your long-term success depends much more on the choices you make during recovery and maintenance than on having a perfect surgery day experience. The goal is to get through this day safely and successfully so you can begin the real work of building the healthy lifestyle that will support your transformation for years to come.

Chapter 6 Make Your Move

These exercises help you prepare mentally and practically for your surgery countdown period, manage pre-surgery anxiety, avoid common pitfalls like the farewell food tour, and approach your surgery day with confidence and readiness for the transformation ahead.

Create your surgery countdown calendar by marking important dates and deadlines for the final weeks before your procedure, including when to start your pre-surgery diet, when to stop certain medications, when to complete pre-operative appointments, and when to begin specific preparations like organizing your recovery space or arranging help from family and friends. Having a clear timeline reduces anxiety about forgetting important tasks and helps you spread preparations over several weeks rather than scrambling at the last minute.

Design your recovery command center by setting up

your main recovery space with everything you'll need within easy reach, including water bottles, protein drinks, medications, entertainment options, comfort items, and anything else that will support your healing and compliance with post-surgery guidelines. Take photos of your setup so you can make adjustments if needed and feel confident that you're prepared for the practical aspects of recovery.

Build your pre-surgery meal plan by researching and preparing foods that meet your pre-surgery diet requirements while also giving you practice with the types of foods you'll eat after surgery. Include protein-rich options, clear liquids, pureed foods, and soft solids so you can experiment with flavors and textures before your taste preferences potentially change after surgery.

Develop your anxiety management toolkit specifically for surgery day by practicing relaxation techniques, positive visualizations, and confidence-building exercises that you can use during waiting periods, medical preparations, and any moments when fear threatens to overwhelm your excitement about your transformation. Write down your most effective techniques so you can reference them when you're feeling nervous.

Create your farewell tour alternative plan by identifying healthy ways to honor your relationship with food without engaging in binge eating or breaking your pre-surgery diet requirements. This might include writing letters to foods you'll eat less frequently, taking photos of meaningful food memories, or planning special post-surgery meals that fit your new eating plan but still feel celebratory.

Establish your support system activation plan by identifying who you'll contact for different types of help during your countdown and recovery periods, including practical support for household tasks, emotional support for encouragement and listening, and informational support for questions about your experience. Share your surgery date with key support people and let them know specifically how they can help you succeed.

Write your surgery day intention statement by describing how you want to feel and behave on your surgery day, what you want to focus on instead of fears and worries, and what mantras or reminders will help you stay calm and confident throughout the process. Include your reasons for choosing surgery and your excitement about the transformation ahead to keep your attention on positive outcomes rather than potential problems.

Finally, prepare your post-surgery success plan by outlining your goals for the first week, first month, and first three months after surgery, including specific eating guidelines you'll follow, support resources you'll use, and milestones you want to achieve. Having concrete plans for your recovery period helps you feel prepared and excited about the journey ahead rather than anxious about the unknown aspects of life after surgery.

Review these preparations regularly during your countdown period and adjust them based on new information from your surgical team or changes in your circumstances. The more thoroughly you prepare for both the practical and emotional aspects of your surgery experience, the more confident and successful you'll feel throughout your transformation journey.

Chapter 7: Your New Normal

The months after weight loss surgery don't look anything like what you imagined during all those weeks of planning and preparing, and nobody warns you that the hardest part isn't the surgery itself but figuring out how to live in a body that changes every single week while everyone around you acts like you should be nothing but grateful and excited about your transformation. You wake up one morning and realize your clothes don't fit, your energy levels are completely different, people treat you like a different person, and you're supposed to navigate all of this while learning to eat in ways that feel foreign and sometimes frustrating.

This becomes your new normal, but normal feels like the wrong word for something that changes so constantly and affects every aspect of how you move through the world.

Your relationship with food shifts from something you could do without thinking to something that requires planning, measuring, and constant attention to how your body responds to different foods and portions. Your social life changes because you can't eat the way you used to at restaurants, family gatherings, and work events, and some people don't know how to relate to the version of you that's emerging as your confidence grows along with your weight loss.

The compliments feel wonderful and terrible at the same time because part of you loves the attention and validation while another part wonders why people treat you better now than they did before, and you start questioning whether relationships are based on how you look rather than who you are as a person. Your identity shifts in ways that feel exciting and unsettling, and you catch yourself in mirrors not recognizing the person looking back at you, which should feel amazing but sometimes just feels confusing.

Learning to live successfully in your new normal requires different skills than getting through surgery and the initial recovery period, because now you're building a life rather than just healing from a procedure, and the choices you make during this adjustment phase determine whether your transformation becomes a lasting change or a temporary improvement that gradually fades as old patterns creep back into your daily routine.

Recovery Reality vs. Expectations

The fantasy version of recovery involves losing weight quickly and easily while feeling amazing and confident from day one, but the reality includes physical discomfort, emotional ups and downs, learning curves with new eating habits, and adjustment periods that nobody mentions in the success stories you read during your research phase. Understanding what recovery actually looks like helps you stay patient with the process instead of panicking when your experience doesn't match the highlight reel versions you've seen from other people.

Your energy levels fluctuate wildly during the first few months as your body adjusts to eating much smaller amounts of food while healing from surgery and losing weight rapidly, and some days you feel like you could conquer the world while other days you can barely get through your normal activities without feeling exhausted.

This energy rollercoaster happens because your body is working hard to heal surgical sites, adapt to new eating patterns, and burn stored fat for energy when you're not consuming enough calories to meet all your daily needs, and the process takes significant energy even though you're not doing anything that feels particularly demanding.

The weight loss itself doesn't happen in a smooth,

predictable line despite what the charts and timelines suggest, and you'll experience weeks where you lose several pounds followed by weeks where the scale doesn't move at all or even goes up slightly, which can trigger panic about whether surgery is working for you or whether you're already failing at something that's supposed to be easier than traditional weight loss methods.

Your relationship with food becomes complicated in ways you didn't expect because you're simultaneously grateful for the tool that helps you eat less and frustrated by the restrictions that make eating feel like work instead of pleasure. Some foods that you used to love now make you feel sick, some textures become intolerable, and you might develop aversions to foods you thought you'd miss terribly after surgery.

The emotional adjustment takes much longer than the physical healing because you're processing the loss of food as your primary comfort while learning new ways to handle stress, boredom, sadness, and celebration, and this transition happens while you're also dealing with a changing body, shifting relationships, and constant attention to your appearance and eating habits from people around you.

Your stomach capacity changes gradually rather than

all at once, and what feels like tiny portions during your first month after surgery might feel like normal amounts by your sixth month, leading to confusion about whether you're eating too much or whether your stomach is stretching back to its original size, when in reality you're experiencing the normal healing process that allows for slightly larger portions over time.

The social aspects of recovery prove more challenging than the medical aspects for many people because you have to navigate restaurants, family dinners, work lunches, and social events while eating portions that look strange to other people and avoiding foods that used to be central to your participation in these activities, and people's reactions range from supportive to curious to judgmental in ways that affect your comfort and confidence.

Your body image adjusts slowly to your changing appearance, and you might still see your pre-surgery body when you look in mirrors or feel surprised when people comment on your weight loss because the changes feel gradual from your perspective even though they appear dramatic to outside observers, leading to a disconnect between how you feel about your appearance and how others perceive your transformation.

The timeline for feeling "normal" in your post-surgery

body varies dramatically from person to person, with some people adapting quickly to their new eating patterns and energy levels while others need six months or more to feel comfortable with their transformed relationship with food and their changing physical capabilities and appearance.

Complications, when they occur, usually involve minor issues like food intolerances, vitamin deficiencies, or temporary digestive problems rather than the major medical emergencies that people fear most, but even minor complications can feel scary when you're already adjusting to so many changes and wondering whether every new symptom indicates a serious problem.

The key to managing recovery reality is adjusting your expectations to include normal variations in energy, weight loss, food tolerance, and emotional adjustment while staying connected to your healthcare team for guidance about what's normal versus what needs medical attention, and remembering that recovery is a process that unfolds over months rather than weeks.

Practice patience with yourself during the adjustment period by celebrating small victories, tracking progress in multiple ways beyond just the scale, and remembering that the skills you're learning now create the foundation for lifelong success rather than just short-term weight loss, so the investment in learning new habits pays dividends for decades rather than just during the initial recovery phase.

Navigating Food Relationships

Building a healthy relationship with food after weight loss surgery requires unlearning decades of emotional eating patterns while simultaneously learning to work with your surgically altered anatomy, and this process involves much more than just following meal plans and protein guidelines because you're fundamentally changing how you think about food, how you use food, and what role food plays in your daily life and emotional wellbeing.

Your new stomach sends different hunger and fullness signals than your pre-surgery anatomy, and learning to interpret these signals accurately takes practice because the sensations feel unfamiliar and sometimes contradictory to what your brain expects based on years of experience with your original stomach capacity and hormone patterns.

The restriction from surgery helps control portions automatically at first, but as your stomach heals and adapts, you need to develop conscious awareness of appropriate portion sizes and eating speeds because eating too quickly or too much can cause discomfort, nausea, or vomiting that makes meals unpleasant rather than satisfying.

Food choices become more important than ever because your smaller stomach capacity means every bite needs to contribute to your nutritional needs rather than just providing pleasure or comfort, and learning to prioritize protein while still enjoying your meals requires creativity and planning that feels overwhelming at first but becomes routine with practice and experience.

The emotional functions that food used to serve in your life need new outlets because you can no longer eat your way through stress, boredom, sadness, or anxiety without physical consequences, and developing alternative coping strategies while you're also adjusting to rapid weight loss and changing relationships creates additional complexity during an already challenging transition period.

Your taste preferences might change after surgery in ways that surprise you, with some people developing aversions to foods they previously loved and new appreciation for foods they used to avoid, and these changes can feel like losing part of your identity if your favorite foods no longer taste good or make you feel sick when you try to eat them.

Social eating becomes more complicated because you can't participate in food-centered activities the way you used to, and you need strategies for handling restaurants, family gatherings, work events, and social situations where your small portions and food restrictions might draw attention or make other people uncomfortable about their own eating habits.

The goal isn't to develop a perfect relationship with food where you never want foods that don't fit your plan or never struggle with emotional eating triggers, but rather to build a sustainable approach where you can enjoy food within the parameters that support your health goals while having reliable alternatives for handling emotions and stress that don't involve eating.

Practice mindful eating by paying attention to hunger and fullness cues, eating slowly without distractions, and focusing on the flavors and textures of your food rather than eating quickly or while watching television, working, or engaging in other activities that prevent you from noticing how food affects your body and satisfaction levels.

Develop a repertoire of go-to meals and snacks that meet your nutritional needs while also tasting good and feeling satisfying, because having reliable options reduces decision fatigue and prevents you from making poor choices when you're hungry and don't have a plan for what to eat that fits your post-surgery requirements.

Create new food traditions and rituals that align with

your transformed eating patterns, such as trying one new healthy recipe each week, having a weekly meal prep session, or celebrating special occasions with high-quality small portions of foods you love rather than large quantities of foods that don't support your goals.

Address emotional eating patterns by identifying your triggers and developing specific alternative responses for each one, because the physical restriction from surgery doesn't eliminate the emotional urges to eat for comfort, and having concrete alternatives ready makes it easier to choose healthier coping strategies when emotions run high.

Build flexibility into your eating plan so you can handle special occasions, travel, and unexpected situations without feeling like you've completely derailed your progress, because rigid rules often lead to all-or-nothing thinking that turns minor deviations into major setbacks rather than normal parts of living a real life with social commitments and changing circumstances.

Remember that developing a healthy relationship with food is an ongoing process rather than a destination you reach and maintain effortlessly, and that setbacks and challenges are normal parts of learning new patterns rather than signs that you're failing or that surgery isn't working for you.

Handling Compliments and Attention

The increased attention that comes with dramatic weight loss feels overwhelming and wonderful at the same time, and learning to handle compliments, comments, and questions about your transformation becomes a crucial skill for maintaining your confidence and protecting your privacy while navigating a world that suddenly treats you very differently than it did when you were heavier.

People notice your weight loss and feel entitled to comment on your body, your eating habits, and your appearance in ways that would be considered rude in any other context, and these comments range from genuine compliments and expressions of concern to intrusive questions and inappropriate observations that make you feel like your body is public property rather than your personal business.

The positive attention can trigger complicated emotions because part of you loves feeling attractive and getting compliments while another part resents the implication that you're more valuable or worthy of attention now than you were at your higher weight, and these conflicted feelings are normal responses to experiencing how differently the world treats people based on their size and appearance.

Some people act like your weight loss gives them permission to discuss your body, your eating choices, and your personal decisions in detail, asking questions about how much you've lost, what you're eating, whether you're done losing weight, and other topics that feel invasive even when they're asked with good intentions and genuine curiosity about your experience.

The comments about looking "too thin" or losing weight "too fast" often come from people who are uncomfortable with dramatic change or who feel threatened by your transformation, and learning to distinguish between genuine concern and projection of other people's fears helps you respond appropriately rather than doubting your progress or your choices.

Coworkers, acquaintances, and even strangers might make assumptions about your weight loss method, your motivations, or your character based on your appearance, and some people will express opinions about weight loss surgery, diet culture, or body image that have nothing to do with your actual experience but everything to do with their own issues and biases.

Develop standard responses to common comments so you're not caught off guard when people ask intrusive questions or make inappropriate observations, and practice delivering these responses with confidence and kindness rather than defensiveness or detailed explanations that invite further discussion of topics you prefer to keep private.

For compliments about your appearance, simple responses like "thank you, I feel great" or "I appreciate that" acknowledge the kindness without opening the door to extended conversations about your weight loss journey, your methods, or your future plans, and they redirect attention to how you feel rather than just how you look.

When people ask about your weight loss method, you can choose to share as much or as little as feels comfortable, with responses ranging from "I'm working with my doctor on a health plan" to "I've made some lifestyle changes" to "I had weight loss surgery and I'm very happy with my decision" depending on your relationship with the person and your comfort level with disclosure.

For comments about losing weight too quickly or looking too thin, responses like "my doctor is monitoring my progress and we're both pleased with my results" or "I'm following medical guidelines and feeling healthier than I have in years" establish that you have professional support and that your weight loss is intentional and medically supervised.

Set boundaries around discussions of your body and your eating habits by redirecting conversations to other topics when people become too focused on your appearance or your food choices, using phrases like "I prefer not to discuss my weight" or "let's talk about something else" when conversations become uncomfortable or invasive.

Practice accepting compliments gracefully rather than deflecting them or minimizing your achievements, because learning to receive positive feedback builds confidence and reinforces your sense of accomplishment, while deflecting compliments can make the person giving them feel dismissed and can reinforce negative self-talk patterns that undermine your progress.

Remember that people's reactions to your transformation often say more about their own issues with weight, body image, and change than they do about your appearance or your choices, and that you don't need to manage other people's discomfort with your success or educate them about weight loss surgery unless you choose to do so.

Focus on how you feel in your body rather than just how you look to other people, because sustainable confidence comes from internal awareness of your health, energy, and capabilities rather than external validation from people who may or may not understand your journey or have your best interests at heart.

Build a support system of people who knew you before surgery and who appreciate you for qualities that have nothing to do with your weight, because these relationships provide stability and perspective during times when the attention and comments from others feel overwhelming or confusing rather than supportive and encouraging.

Staying Connected to Your Why

The initial excitement and motivation that carried you through surgery preparation and early recovery eventually fades as weight loss becomes routine and the daily work of maintaining new habits feels less thrilling than it did when everything was new and dramatic changes were happening quickly, and staying connected to your original reasons for choosing surgery becomes crucial for long-term success when motivation fluctuates and challenges arise.

Your "why" evolves as you achieve some goals and discover new ones, and the reasons that motivated you to have surgery might feel less urgent when you're no longer dealing with the health problems, mobility limitations, or self-confidence issues that originally drove your decision to pursue surgical intervention for your weight struggles.

The honeymoon phase of rapid weight loss and constant compliments gives way to a maintenance phase where progress slows down, attention decreases, and the work of sustaining your new lifestyle becomes more about discipline and routine than excitement and novelty, and this transition challenges many people's ability to stay committed to the habits that created their success.

Plateaus in weight loss are normal and expected parts of the process, but they can trigger panic about whether surgery is still working and whether you're doing something wrong, especially if you've been conditioned by diet culture to expect linear progress and to interpret any stall as evidence of failure rather than a normal part of your body's adjustment to its new weight.

Life stresses, relationship changes, work pressures, and other challenges that have nothing to do with your weight loss journey can affect your ability to maintain the focus and energy required for meal planning, regular exercise, vitamin compliance, and other habits that support your surgical success, and having strategies for maintaining your health priorities during difficult times prevents temporary setbacks from becoming permanent derailments.

The goals that motivated your surgery decision might shift as you achieve them and discover new possibilities for your life that weren't visible when you were focused primarily on losing weight and improving your health, and staying flexible about your motivations while remaining committed to the underlying value of taking care of yourself helps you navigate these transitions successfully.

Reconnect with your original motivations regularly by reviewing the goals you wrote down before surgery, looking at before photos that remind you of how you felt in your pre-surgery body, and reflecting on the health improvements, increased energy, and enhanced quality of life that you've gained through your transformation, even when those benefits start to feel normal rather than miraculous.

Update your goals and motivations as your life changes and new possibilities emerge, because staying connected to your why doesn't mean being stuck with the same reasons forever, but rather maintaining awareness of what matters most to you and how your health choices support or undermine those priorities as they evolve over time.

Create visual reminders of your progress and your

goals by keeping before and after photos visible, maintaining a list of activities you can now do that you couldn't do before surgery, and documenting improvements in your health markers, energy levels, and overall quality of life that go beyond just the number on the scale.

Build accountability systems that help you stay connected to your goals during times when motivation feels low, such as regular check-ins with your healthcare team, participation in support groups, partnerships with workout buddies, or tracking systems that help you monitor your compliance with healthy habits rather than just your weight loss results.

Practice gratitude for your surgical tool and your transformed life by regularly acknowledging the positive changes you've experienced, the opportunities that are now available to you, and the health improvements that surgery has made possible, because focusing on what you've gained rather than what you've given up reinforces your commitment to maintaining the lifestyle that supports your success.

Address challenges and setbacks by reconnecting with your why rather than abandoning your goals, using difficult times as opportunities to recommit to your health priorities and to problem-solve obstacles rather than giving up on the habits and choices that have served you well throughout your transformation journey.

Remember that your why doesn't have to be dramatic or inspiring to other people, it just has to be meaningful enough to you to motivate consistent action even when you don't feel like following through on healthy choices, and that the cumulative effect of small daily decisions aligned with your values creates lasting change more effectively than sporadic bursts of perfect behavior.

Celebrate the person you've become through this process rather than just the weight you've lost, acknowledging the courage it took to have surgery, the discipline you've developed in changing your habits, the resilience you've shown in handling challenges, and the commitment you've demonstrated to prioritizing your health and wellbeing even when it required significant effort and sacrifice.

Chapter 7 Make Your Move

These exercises help you adjust to life after weight loss surgery by setting realistic expectations, developing healthy food relationships, preparing for increased attention, maintaining long-term motivation, and building sustainable habits that support your transformed lifestyle for years to come.

Create your recovery reality tracker by documenting your actual experiences during the first six months after surgery, including energy levels, weight loss patterns, food tolerances, emotional changes, and social situations, so you can identify what's normal for your individual journey rather than comparing your experience to idealized timelines or other people's results. Update this tracker weekly to notice patterns and progress that might not be obvious from day to day.

Develop your food relationship assessment by evaluating your current eating patterns, emotional triggers, social eating challenges, and satisfaction levels with your post-surgery diet, then identify specific areas where you want to build healthier habits or address ongoing struggles with food choices, portion control, or emotional eating patterns that surgery didn't automatically resolve.

Build your compliment and attention response script by writing down standard responses to common comments about your weight loss, appearance, eating habits, and surgery decision, then practice delivering these responses with confidence and appropriate boundaries so you're prepared for various social situations without feeling caught off guard or pressured to share more than you're comfortable discussing.

Update your motivation and goals document by reviewing your original reasons for having surgery and identifying which goals you've achieved, which ones remain important, and what new motivations have emerged as your life has changed, then create specific action plans for staying connected to these evolving reasons during times when motivation feels low or challenges arise.

Design your plateau and challenge management plan by identifying strategies for handling weight loss stalls, life stresses that affect your eating habits, social pressures that challenge your healthy choices, and other obstacles that could derail your progress, including specific people to contact for support and concrete actions to take when you feel your commitment wavering.

Establish your long-term success monitoring system by choosing specific metrics beyond weight loss to track your ongoing health and wellbeing, such as energy levels, physical capabilities, health markers, mood stability, and life satisfaction, so you can maintain perspective on your overall progress even during times when the scale doesn't reflect your efforts.

Create your new normal celebration plan by identifying ways to acknowledge your transformation that don't involve food, including activities you can now participate in, clothes you can now wear, experiences you can now enjoy, and accomplishments you can now pursue that weren't possible at your pre-surgery weight, and schedule regular celebrations of these non-scale victories.

Finally, build your support system maintenance strategy by evaluating your current support network and identifying any gaps in practical help, emotional encouragement, or informational resources, then create plans for staying connected with supportive people, finding new sources of help as your needs change, and contributing support to others who are earlier in their weight loss surgery journey.

Review and adjust these action plans regularly as your new normal continues to evolve, because the skills and strategies that serve you during your first year after surgery might need modification as you move into long-term maintenance and face different challenges and opportunities in your transformed life.

Chapter 8: Living with Guts, Grace & Grit

You made it through surgery, survived the recovery phase, learned to eat in ways that felt impossible at first, handled the compliments and the criticism, and figured out how to live in a body that changes every month while everyone around you adjusts to the person you're becoming. The dramatic weight loss phase might be slowing down, the initial excitement has settled into routine, and now you're facing the real question that determines whether this transformation lasts for years or becomes another temporary change that gradually fades back into old patterns.

The question isn't whether you can lose weight with surgery, because you've already proven that you can.

The question is whether you can build a life you love in your transformed body, whether you can maintain the habits that created your success when motivation fluctuates and life gets complicated, whether you can show up fully in the world instead of hiding behind old insecurities, and whether you can use your experience to help other people find their own courage to change their lives.

This phase of your journey requires different skills than getting through surgery or learning new eating habits, because now you're not just maintaining weight loss, you're creating a legacy of courage and resilience that affects everyone around you. You're modeling what it looks like to take control of your health, to invest in yourself without apology, to handle criticism with grace, and to keep growing even when the path gets difficult.

Living with guts, grace, and grit means owning your transformation completely, celebrating your courage without minimizing your achievement, supporting other people who are struggling with the same challenges you've overcome, and building a life that honors the investment you made in yourself through surgery while continuing to grow in ways that have nothing to do with the number on the scale.

Embracing Your Transformation

Owning your success means accepting that you deserve the life you've created through surgery and the hard work that followed, and this acceptance proves harder than losing the weight for many people because it requires believing that you're worthy of health, happiness, and all the opportunities that come with feeling confident in your body and proud of your choices.

You might catch yourself minimizing your achievement when people compliment your transformation, deflecting praise by talking about how surgery did all the work or how you still have more weight to lose or how you don't look that different, but these responses rob you of the satisfaction that comes from acknowledging your courage and commitment throughout this process.

The truth is that surgery gave you a tool, but you did the work of using that tool effectively every single day through meal planning, protein prioritizing, vitamin taking, exercise scheduling, relationship navigating, and all the other choices that determine whether surgical tools create lasting change or temporary improvement.

You chose to have surgery when staying the same felt more dangerous than facing the unknown, and that choice required courage that most people never have to summon because they've never faced the health risks, mobility limitations, and quality of life restrictions that come with significant obesity.

You prepared for surgery by researching procedures, choosing medical teams, arranging time off work, organizing childcare, and handling a thousand other details while managing your own fears and other people's opinions about your decision to prioritize your health over their comfort with your previous size.

You recovered from surgery by following eating guidelines that felt restrictive and strange, taking vitamins that made you nauseous, attending follow-up appointments when you felt fine, and trusting a process that required patience when you wanted immediate results and certainty when everything felt unpredictable.

You learned new eating habits by planning every meal, measuring every portion, prioritizing protein over foods you preferred, eating slowly when you wanted to eat quickly, and stopping when you felt satisfied instead of when you felt full, and you maintained these habits even when they felt tedious and socially awkward.

You handled relationship changes by setting boundaries with people who undermined your progress, educating family members about your new requirements, finding new ways to socialize that didn't revolve around food, and maintaining connections with people who supported your transformation while limiting contact with those who didn't.

You navigated identity changes by figuring out who you are in a smaller body, learning to accept compliments about your appearance, building confidence that doesn't depend on other people's approval, and staying connected to your values and personality while everything else about your life was shifting.

You persisted through plateaus, setbacks, and challenges by recommitting to your goals when motivation felt low, problem-solving obstacles instead of giving up, seeking help when you needed it, and treating mistakes as learning opportunities rather than evidence that you were failing at something that should be easier.

Every single day that you choose foods that support your goals instead of foods that provide temporary comfort, every time you exercise when you'd rather stay on the couch, every moment you speak up for yourself instead of accepting treatment you don't deserve, and every decision you make to prioritize your health and happiness demonstrates the guts, grace, and grit that created your transformation.

Embracing your transformation means celebrating these daily choices as evidence of your strength and commitment rather than dismissing them as things you're supposed to do or minimizing them because they've become routine parts of your lifestyle.

Practice owning your success by accepting compliments gracefully, sharing your story when it might help someone else, wearing clothes that show your figure instead of hiding it, participating in activities you avoided at higher weights, and treating yourself with the same respect and admiration you would show anyone else who had accomplished what you've accomplished.

Remember that your transformation inspires other people to believe that change is possible in their own lives, and that minimizing your achievement robs them of the hope and motivation they might gain from seeing your success and understanding the work and courage it required.

Your transformation matters not just because you lost weight, but because you proved that people can change their lives dramatically when they're willing to use available tools, do the necessary work, and persist through challenges that would stop most people from reaching their goals.

Paying It Forward

Sharing your story and supporting other people who are considering or preparing for weight loss surgery deepens your own healing by giving meaning to your struggles and creating connections with people who understand your journey in ways that family and friends who haven't faced similar challenges simply cannot relate to or fully appreciate.

You have wisdom that can only come from living through the experience of choosing surgery, preparing for transformation, recovering from the procedure, learning new habits, handling relationship changes, and building a life you love in your transformed body, and this wisdom becomes valuable to other people who are facing the same fears and challenges you've already overcome.

The questions that kept you awake before surgery, the doubts that made you second-guess your decision, the fears about complications and failure, the concerns about relationship changes and identity shifts, and the practical challenges of learning new eating habits are the same issues that torture other people who are considering the same path you chose.

Your perspective as someone who has walked this path successfully provides hope and practical guidance that medical professionals, family members, and friends cannot offer because they haven't experienced the emotional complexity, the physical challenges, and the social navigation required to succeed with weight loss surgery.

Paying it forward doesn't require becoming a professional counselor or dedicating your life to helping other people, but it does mean being willing to share your experience honestly when opportunities arise and someone could benefit from your perspective and encouragement.

This might involve participating in support groups where pre-surgery patients can ask questions and hear from people who have succeeded long-term, sharing your story on social media platforms where people research surgery options, volunteering at information sessions hosted by surgical programs, or simply being open about your experience when friends, coworkers, or acquaintances express interest in learning more about weight loss surgery.

The most valuable gift you can offer other people is honesty about both the challenges and the benefits of surgery, because the people who succeed long-term are those who approach the process with realistic expectations rather than fantasies about easy transformation or fears about impossible lifestyle changes.

Share the practical details that nobody talks about during surgery preparation, like how to handle social situations during the early recovery phase, what foods work best during different stages of healing, how to manage energy fluctuations during rapid weight loss, and what relationship changes to expect as your confidence grows and your priorities shift.

Be honest about the ongoing work required for long-term success, including the daily discipline of meal planning and protein prioritizing, the social navigation required when you can't eat the way other people eat, the mental work of building confidence and handling attention, and the commitment required to maintain healthy habits when motivation fluctuates and life gets complicated.

Acknowledge the emotional challenges that surgery doesn't automatically solve, such as learning new coping strategies when food is no longer your primary comfort, handling grief about losing familiar eating patterns, navigating identity changes as your body and confidence transform, and maintaining motivation during plateau periods when progress stalls.

Emphasize the positive aspects of transformation that go beyond weight loss, including increased energy for activities and relationships, improved health markers and reduced medication needs, enhanced confidence and self-advocacy skills, and the satisfaction that comes from proving to yourself that you can make dramatic positive changes when you're willing to use effective tools and do the necessary work.

Connect people with resources that supported your success, such as specific support groups, helpful books like this one, websites, and practical tools for meal planning, exercise, and habit tracking that made your journey easier and more sustainable.

Remember that your story provides hope for people who feel hopeless about their ability to change their health and their lives, and that sharing your experience honestly and compassionately can be the encouragement someone needs to take action that dramatically improves their quality of life and potentially saves their life.

Supporting other people also reinforces your own commitment to maintaining the lifestyle that created your success, because teaching and encouraging others requires you to stay connected to the principles and practices that support long-term surgical success.

The community you build with other people who have shared similar experiences provides ongoing support for your own journey while creating meaningful relationships based on mutual understanding, shared challenges, and collective wisdom about navigating life after weight loss surgery.

Maintaining Your Mental Health

Protecting your emotional wellbeing becomes a lifelong practice that requires ongoing attention and adjustment as your life circumstances change, your relationships evolve, and new challenges arise that test your resilience and coping skills in ways that have nothing to do with your weight but everything to do with your ability to maintain the healthy habits that support your surgical success.

The mental health challenges that contributed to your weight struggles don't automatically disappear when you lose weight, and some issues become more apparent when you can no longer use food to numb difficult emotions or avoid dealing with problems that feel overwhelming or scary.

Depression, anxiety, trauma, relationship problems, work stress, and other mental health concerns require attention and treatment regardless of your weight, and maintaining your physical transformation depends partly on addressing these underlying issues that can trigger old coping patterns if they remain unresolved.

The identity changes that come with dramatic weight loss can create new mental health challenges even when you're happy with your physical transformation, because adjusting to a different body, different social reactions, and different capabilities requires psychological flexibility and self-compassion during periods of confusion and adjustment.

Body image issues don't automatically resolve when you reach your goal weight, and some people struggle with accepting their transformed appearance, dealing with loose skin or other physical changes, or feeling comfortable with attention and compliments about their appearance after years of feeling invisible or criticized.

Relationship changes that accompany weight loss can create stress, grief, and conflict that affect your emotional stability and your ability to maintain healthy habits, especially when important relationships become strained or when you outgrow friendships that were based on shared complaints about weight and body image rather than genuine connection and mutual support.

The pressure to maintain your weight loss and continue making healthy choices can create anxiety and perfectionist thinking that makes normal fluctuations in weight, energy, or motivation feel like failures rather than natural parts of living a real life with changing circumstances and competing priorities.

Building long-term mental health strategies starts with recognizing that emotional wellbeing requires the same ongoing attention and investment as physical health, and that maintaining good mental health supports your ability to make choices that align with your values and goals rather than being driven by emotions, impulses, or external pressures.

Develop stress management techniques that don't involve food, such as regular exercise, meditation or prayer, creative hobbies, social connections, time in nature, or other activities that provide relief and perspective when life feels overwhelming or when you're tempted to return to old coping patterns that don't serve your goals.

Build a support network that includes professional mental health resources such as counselors who understand the psychological aspects of weight loss surgery, support groups for people who have had similar experiences, and healthcare providers who can address both your physical and emotional needs as they change over time.

Practice self-compassion during setbacks and challenges by treating yourself with the same kindness you would show a good friend who was struggling, recognizing that perfection isn't required for success, and viewing mistakes as learning opportunities rather than evidence that you're failing or that surgery isn't working for you.

Maintain perspective on your overall progress by tracking multiple measures of success beyond just weight loss, including improvements in health markers, energy levels, physical capabilities, confidence, relationships, and life satisfaction that demonstrate the positive impact of your transformation even during periods when the scale doesn't reflect your efforts.

Address new challenges proactively rather than waiting until they become overwhelming, whether these involve relationship problems, work stress, health concerns, or other life circumstances that could affect your ability to maintain the habits and mindset that support your surgical success.

Stay connected to activities and relationships that bring you joy and meaning beyond your weight loss journey, because having a rich, fulfilling life that includes multiple sources of satisfaction and identity makes you more resilient during difficult times and less likely to define your worth entirely by your appearance or your eating habits.

Remember that seeking help for mental health concerns demonstrates strength and wisdom rather than weakness, and that addressing emotional challenges early prevents them from escalating into problems that could derail your physical health progress or your overall quality of life.

Living Fully in Your New Body

Taking up space and showing up fully in your transformed life requires unlearning years of hiding, shrinking, and making yourself smaller to accommodate other people's comfort, and this process of expansion and visibility often feels scarier than the surgery itself because it requires vulnerability and confidence that you might not have practiced when you were using your weight as a shield or an excuse to avoid certain experiences and opportunities.

Your new body can do things that your pre-surgery body couldn't do, but stepping into these new capabilities requires mental courage as well as physical ability because you have to overcome years of conditioning that taught you to avoid activities, decline invitations, and limit your participation based on assumptions about what your body could handle or how you would look doing certain things.

The clothes that fit your transformed body might feel strange and exposing after years of choosing outfits based on camouflaging your size rather than expressing your personality or showing your figure, and learning to dress your new body with confidence requires experimenting with styles, colors, and fits that you avoided when you felt self-conscious about your appearance.

Social situations that used to feel uncomfortable because of your weight might still trigger anxiety because the mental habits of self-consciousness and social avoidance don't automatically disappear when your body changes, and building confidence in group settings requires practice and patience as you learn to trust that you belong in spaces where you previously felt out of place.

Physical activities that were difficult or impossible at your higher weight become accessible as you lose weight and gain energy, but trying new activities requires overcoming fears about your capabilities, concerns about how you'll look, and anxiety about being judged by other people who might not understand your journey or your previous limitations.

The attention that comes with your transformed appearance might feel overwhelming even when it's positive, because learning to be visible and to accept compliments gracefully requires different skills than blending into the background and deflecting attention, and this transition can feel vulnerable and uncomfortable even when you're happy with your results.

Professional opportunities might expand as your confidence grows and your energy increases, but pursuing promotions, speaking up in meetings, or taking on leadership roles requires believing that you deserve success and recognition rather than staying in the background where you felt safer when you were less confident about your appearance and capabilities.

Romantic relationships might change or become possible in new ways as your confidence and attractiveness increase, but opening yourself to intimacy and connection requires vulnerability and self-acceptance that goes beyond just losing weight, because healthy relationships depend on believing that you're worthy of love and respect regardless of your size.

Living fully means saying yes to invitations you would have declined, trying activities you avoided, wearing clothes that show your figure, speaking up when you have something to contribute, and taking up the space you deserve in every area of your life rather than shrinking to accommodate other people's expectations or your own outdated beliefs about what you're capable of or worthy of experiencing.

Challenge yourself to try one new activity each month that you avoided at your higher weight, whether this involves physical activities like hiking or dancing, social activities like parties or networking events, or personal challenges like public speaking or creative pursuits that require confidence and visibility.

Practice taking up space in small ways that build your confidence for bigger challenges, such as sitting in the front row at events, speaking up in meetings, wearing bright colors, or participating in conversations where you previously would have stayed quiet and let other people lead the discussion.

Build a wardrobe that reflects your personality and makes you feel confident rather than just buying smaller versions of the clothes you wore when you were hiding your body, and experiment with styles, colors, and fits that show your figure and express who you are rather than who you think you should be.

Seek out experiences and opportunities that were difficult or impossible at your higher weight, such as traveling to places that required significant walking, attending events in small spaces, or participating in activities that have weight limits or physical requirements that you can now meet.

Remember that you earned the right to live fully through the courage it took to have surgery and the discipline it took to maintain your transformation, and that hiding your success or minimizing your capabilities dishonors the investment you made in yourself and limits the inspiration you could provide to other people who are struggling with similar challenges.

Your visibility and confidence give other people permission to believe that transformation is possible and that they deserve to live fully in their own bodies, regardless of their current size or their previous limitations, and this ripple effect multiplies the positive impact of your personal transformation beyond just your own life and happiness.

Chapter 8 Make Your Move

These exercises help you fully embrace your transformation, develop ways to support others on similar journeys, create long-term mental health strategies, and commit to living boldly in your transformed body while continuing to grow in ways that honor your courage and investment in yourself.

Create your transformation celebration inventory by listing specific achievements, improvements, and positive changes you've experienced since surgery, including health improvements, increased activities, enhanced confidence, better relationships, and new opportunities that weren't available at your higher weight, then plan specific ways to acknowledge and celebrate these accomplishments that don't involve food but do honor the magnitude of what you've achieved.

Develop your story-sharing strategy by writing down the key points of your weight loss surgery journey that might help other people, including your decision-making process, preparation strategies, recovery experiences, challenges you've overcome, and lessons you've learned, then identify specific ways you're comfortable sharing this information, such as support groups, social media, informal conversations, or volunteer opportunities with surgical programs.

Build your mental health maintenance plan by assessing your current emotional wellbeing, identifying potential stress triggers and coping challenges, listing professional and personal support resources you can access when needed, and creating specific strategies for managing anxiety, depression, relationship stress, and other mental health concerns that could affect your ability to maintain healthy habits long-term.

Design your visibility and confidence expansion plan by identifying activities, opportunities, and experiences you've avoided due to weight-related concerns, then create specific goals for trying new things, taking up more space, and showing up more fully in your personal and professional life, including timelines and support systems that will help you follow through on these commitments to yourself.

Establish your ongoing growth goals by identifying areas of your life beyond weight loss where you want to continue developing, such as career advancement, relationship improvement, creative pursuits, physical challenges, or personal interests that you can now pursue with increased energy and confidence, and create specific action plans for making progress in these areas.

Create your support and mentorship opportunities assessment by identifying ways you can help other people who are considering or recovering from weight loss surgery, such as participating in support groups, volunteering with surgical programs, sharing your story online, or simply being open about your experience when people ask questions, and commit to specific actions that feel comfortable and meaningful to you.

Build your long-term success monitoring system by identifying specific metrics and check-in practices that will help you maintain your physical and emotional health over the years ahead, including regular healthcare appointments, mental health resources, support group participation, and personal reflection practices that keep you connected to your goals and values as your life continues to evolve.

Finally, write a letter to yourself five years in the future describing the life you want to be living, the person you want to have become, the impact you want to have had on other people, and the legacy you want to create through your transformation, then create specific commitments and action steps that will help you become that person and live that life with the guts, grace, and grit that brought you this far on your journey.

Review and update these action plans annually as your life circumstances change and new opportunities for growth and contribution emerge, because the transformation you've achieved through surgery is just the beginning of a lifetime of continued growth, service, and living fully in the body and life you've created through your courage and commitment to your health and happiness.

Stay the Course

Your Journey of Courage

You started this journey terrified and uncertain, wondering if you were making the biggest mistake of your life or the best decision you'd ever make, and now you know the answer. You've proven to yourself and everyone around you that choosing weight loss surgery wasn't about being broken or taking shortcuts, it was about being brave enough to use every tool available to create the life you deserve, and that courage has transformed more than just your body.

The person who picked up this book months ago, scared and full of doubt about whether surgery was the right choice, bears little resemblance to the person reading these words now.

You've learned to eat in ways that felt impossible at first, navigated relationship changes that nobody warned you about, handled compliments and criticism with equal grace, and built confidence that doesn't depend on other people's approval or the number on a scale. You've discovered strength you didn't know you had, developed skills you never thought you'd need, and created a life that honors the investment you made in yourself through surgery.

The fear that used to control your decisions has been replaced by wisdom earned through experience. The shame that kept you hiding has been replaced by pride in your accomplishments. The doubt that made you question every choice has been replaced by trust in your ability to handle whatever challenges come your way, because you've already handled the biggest challenge of all: completely transforming your relationship with food, your body, and yourself.

Your journey required guts to make hard choices when everyone had opinions about your body, grace to forgive yourself for imperfection while handling others' reactions with kindness, and grit to keep going when motivation faded and the real work of maintenance began. These qualities weren't given to you by surgery, they were developed through every difficult decision, every uncomfortable conversation, and every moment you chose your health over other people's comfort.

The courage you've shown inspires other people to believe that dramatic change is possible in their own lives. Your willingness to prioritize your health gives others permission to do the same. Your success proves that people can transform their lives when they're willing to use effective tools, do the necessary work, and persist through challenges that would stop most people from reaching their goals.

You've become living proof that weight loss surgery isn't the easy way out, it's the way that works when you're ready to do the work. You've demonstrated that asking for help shows strength rather than weakness, that using available tools demonstrates wisdom rather than failure, and that investing in your health benefits everyone who cares about you rather than being selfish or vain.

The identity shifts that felt so scary during your transformation have revealed who you really are beneath the weight that used to define you. You're still the same person who loves your family, cares about your friends, and holds the same values about what matters in life, but now you show up fully instead of hiding, speak up instead of staying silent, and take up the space you deserve instead of shrinking to make others comfortable.

Time to Show Up for Yourself

The tools you've developed throughout this journey have prepared you for more than just maintaining weight loss, they've equipped you with emotional resilience, practical skills, and unshakeable confidence that will serve you in every area of your life for decades to come. You now know how to set boundaries that protect your peace, challenge thoughts that undermine your confidence, and navigate relationships that support your growth rather than sabotage your success.

You've learned to separate your worth from your weight, your value from other people's opinions, and your happiness from external validation that can disappear as quickly as it appears.

The confidence you've built doesn't depend on perfect eating, ideal weight maintenance, or constant compliments from others, because it's rooted in your proven ability to make hard choices, overcome obstacles, and create positive change even when the path feels uncertain and the outcome isn't guaranteed.

Your relationship with food has evolved from something that controlled your thoughts and emotions to something that nourishes your body and supports your goals without dominating your mental energy or determining your mood. You've developed the ability to eat for fuel and pleasure without using food as your primary source of comfort, entertainment, or emotional regulation.

The social skills you've practiced while navigating

comments about your transformation, questions about your eating habits, and changes in how people treat you have made you more assertive, more diplomatic, and more skilled at protecting your emotional wellbeing while maintaining important relationships that support your happiness and success.

You've discovered that showing up for yourself doesn't mean being selfish or inconsiderate of others, it means taking responsibility for your own happiness and health so you can be fully present and genuinely helpful to the people you love. The energy you used to spend worrying about your weight, planning your next diet, or avoiding activities because of your size is now available for pursuing goals, building relationships, and contributing to causes that matter to you.

The practical strategies you've mastered for meal planning, stress management, exercise consistency, and habit maintenance have created a foundation of daily practices that support not just your physical health but your mental clarity, emotional stability, and overall life satisfaction in ways that extend far beyond weight management.

Your ability to handle setbacks without turning them into complete derailments, to bounce back from mistakes without spiraling into shame and self-criticism, and to adjust your approach when something isn't working demonstrates resilience that will serve you through every challenge and transition you face in the years ahead.

The support network you've built includes people who knew you before your transformation and people who've met you since, creating a community of relationships based on mutual respect, shared values, and genuine care rather than superficial connections that depend on your appearance or your ability to make others comfortable with their own choices.

You've proven to yourself that you can trust your instincts, make difficult decisions, and follow through on commitments even when motivation fluctuates and circumstances change. This self-trust becomes the foundation for every future goal you set, every challenge you face, and every opportunity you choose to pursue or decline based on what aligns with your values and priorities.

The person you've become through this process deserves to live fully, love deeply, and pursue dreams that might have felt impossible when you were carrying extra weight and the emotional burden that came with it. You've earned the right to take up space, speak your truth, and expect treatment that reflects your worth rather than accepting less because you don't believe you deserve better.

Your Guts, Grace & Grit Action Plan

Moving forward from this transformation requires implementing everything you've learned by trusting your decision completely, setting firm boundaries consistently, building daily confidence habits systematically, and showing up fully for the amazing life you're creating through your continued commitment to growth, health, and authentic self-expression.

Trusting your decision means never again apologizing for choosing surgery, minimizing your success to make others comfortable, or second-guessing the choice that gave you your life back. You researched thoroughly, chose carefully, prepared extensively, and followed through courageously, and the results speak for themselves in your improved health, increased energy, enhanced confidence, and expanded possibilities for how you want to spend your time and energy in the years ahead.

When people question your choice or suggest you could have achieved the same results through willpower alone, remind yourself that you tried those methods for years without lasting success, and that choosing the most effective tool available demonstrates wisdom and self-advocacy rather than weakness or failure. Your decision was based on evidence, medical guidance, and realistic assessment of what works for long-term weight management, not on impulse or wishful thinking.

Set firm boundaries means protecting your mental space, your physical health, and your emotional wellbeing from people and situations that drain your energy or undermine your progress toward continued growth and happiness. This includes limiting time with people who consistently make negative comments about your appearance, your eating habits, or your lifestyle choices, even when those people are family members or longtime friends who claim to care about your wellbeing.

Your boundaries also include saying no to social obligations that don't align with your values, declining invitations to events that center around unhealthy behaviors, and refusing to engage in conversations that focus on criticizing other people's bodies, food choices, or life decisions because these discussions reinforce toxic attitudes that don't support anyone's wellbeing or happiness.

Building daily confidence habits means creating routines and practices that reinforce your sense of worth, capability, and deserving of good things regardless of external circumstances or other people's reactions to your choices and achievements. This might include morning affirmations that remind you of your strength and progress, evening gratitude practices that acknowledge positive experiences and accomplishments, or weekly activities that challenge you to try new things and expand your comfort zone.

Your confidence habits also include taking care of your appearance in ways that make you feel attractive and put-together, not because your worth depends on how you look but because feeling good about your appearance supports your overall confidence and willingness to show up fully in social and professional situations where you want to make positive impressions.

Showing up fully means participating actively in your own life instead of watching from the sidelines, contributing your talents and perspectives instead of staying quiet and letting others lead, and pursuing opportunities that excite you instead of making excuses about why you're not ready or qualified or deserving of success and recognition.

This includes applying for jobs or promotions that interest you, joining groups or organizations that align with your values, traveling to places you've always wanted to visit, trying activities that challenge you physically or mentally, and building relationships with people who inspire you to grow and become the best version of yourself.

Your action plan also includes continuing to pay it forward by sharing your story with people who might benefit from your experience, supporting others who are earlier in their weight loss surgery journey, and using your transformation as evidence that dramatic positive change is possible when people are willing to use effective tools and do the necessary work to create the lives they want.

The ripple effects of your courage extend far beyond your personal transformation because your success gives other people permission to believe that they too can overcome obstacles, change patterns that aren't serving them, and invest in their health and happiness without guilt or apology for prioritizing their own wellbeing.

Your commitment to continued growth means never becoming complacent about your health habits, your relationship skills, or your personal development, but instead viewing your surgical success as the foundation for a lifetime of learning, growing, and contributing to causes and relationships that matter to you.

The guts that got you through surgery becomes the courage to pursue new challenges and opportunities. The grace that helped you handle criticism and relationship changes becomes the wisdom to treat yourself and others with compassion during difficult times. The grit that sustained you through plateaus and setbacks becomes the persistence to maintain healthy habits and positive attitudes even when motivation fluctuates and life gets complicated.

You've already proven you have everything it takes to succeed at the most challenging transformation most people ever attempt, and that same strength, wisdom, and determination will serve you through every adventure, challenge, and opportunity that lies ahead in the amazing life you've created through your courage to change everything.

www.ingramcontent.com/pod-product-compliance
Lightning Source LLC
Chambersburg PA
CBHW061748120626
46550CB00005B/1924